DESIGN KNITTING

DESIGN KNITTING

Marianne Ake
Barbara Baker
Dione Christensen
Phoebe Fox
Maria Hart
Linda Mendelson
Andrée Rubin
and Monna Weinman

edited by Mark Dittrick

photographs by Jeffrey Fox

HAWTHORN BOOKS, INC.
Publishers/NEW YORK
A Howard & Wyndham Company

Library of Congress Catalog Card Number: 78–53411

ISBN: 0–8015–2021–5

1 2 3 4 5 6 7 8 9 10

Contents

List of Abbreviations

approx = approximately
arnd = around
att = attach
beg = beginning
ch = chain
ch st = chain stitch
cont = continue
CC = contrasting color
dec = decrease
det = detach
dc = double crochet
dp = double-point
inc = increase
k = knit
k 1-inc 1 = knit in front and back of stitch
lp = loop
m 1 dbl = make 1 (wool twice around needle)
psso = pass slip stitch over

patt = pattern
patt st = pattern stitch
p = purl
rem = remaining
rnd = round
sc = single crochet
sk = skip
skpo = slip 1, knit 1, psso
sl = slip
sl st = slip stitch
st(s) = stitch(es)
st st = stockinette stitch
tbl = through back loop
tog = together
wrn = wool around needle
wyif = with yarn in front of work
yo = yarn over (to make one stitch)

Yarns noted in instructions are given generically. Unusual or special yarns and the addresses of their manufacturers or distributors are given in the back of the book.

Preface

Interest in knitting has continued to grow ever since the invention of the knitting frame nearly two thousand years ago.

Design Knitting, a lavish compendium of unique fashion designs, bears witness to the fact that the craft is more exciting today than ever before. Here for the first time in a single book is gathered together an impressive array of top knitting design talent. The authors, Marianne Ake, Barbara Baker, Dione Christensen, Phoebe Fox, Maria Hart, Linda Mendelson, Andrée Rubin, and Monna Weinman are the authors; they created the designs and wrote the instructions.

And all the designs are completely original; none of them has ever been published anywhere else before. There are garments worked with unusual combinations of yarns, something rarely seen in even the best needlework publications. Moreover, unlike those frequently out-of-date designs found in books that are merely collections of projects taken from old issues of magazines, the work in Design Knitting is contemporary, reflecting the very latest fashion trends. In fact, what you'll find here is nothing short of the best and most original work of eight of the best knitters now working in America.

None of us was around when the knitting frame was invented, or when the first knitting needles appeared, or when the first knitting machine was unveiled, but luckily there is one knitting milestone we can all share in—Design Knitting. I am proud to have had something to do with it.

Mark Dittrick

Marianne Ake

Marianne Ake learned to knit at school in Sweden, where knitting is compulsory for thirteen-year-old girls. "The first thing everyone makes," she says, "is mittens. Then we had to make baby clothes—at thirteen! We were hardly more than babies ourselves then." Marianne hasn't stopped knitting since, and her long and creative career has encompassed designing, retailing, and producing garments and designs for leading magazines, including Woman's Day, Family Circle, and McCall's. In one four-year period numerous items appeared in magazines under her name.

"Some people call my things high fashion, but that is not really the kind of designing I want to do. I feel that only a few people can wear truly high fashion garments, so I try to design my knits to suit everybody. I am interested in fashion, of course, but also in practicality; and if my clothes look good on most women—not just on beautiful, slim models—I am happy.

"More important, however, I feel that hand-knits should look as different as possible from machine-made garments. Making something that might just as well have been made in a factory seems pointless and therefore I try to make clothes that cannot easily be mass-produced. When I plan a knit, I want at least one of three things to be new, different, and quite interesting: either the yarn, or the style of the garment, or the stitch pattern. The easiest way to keep knits from looking machine-made is to choose a yarn that machines cannot (yet) knit—yarns with bumps or long hairs. The best styles are usually the least complex but with added details according to the fashion of the day—collars, cuffs, pockets, drawstrings, etc. Currently, I am most interested in stitch patterns. After many years of knitting, I am beginning to realize how very complex knitting is—if one wants it to be. Juggling stitches about and experimenting with gauge offers unlimited design possibilities. Today I am totally fascinated by this craft."

Marianne Ake

Rose Chenille Vest

Sizes and Measurements:

Chest: Sizes 6 and 8 measure 31″, size 10, 33½″, and sizes 12 and 14, 35¼″.

The length of vest is 19″ from back neck to lower edge in all sizes.

Materials:

6-Cut cotton chenille, 10 (11, 12) oz.

6 Buttons, ½″ in diameter.

Needles:

Size 10½, or size to obtain gauge.

Gauge:

3 sts = 1″, 5 garter st rows = 1″.

BACK:

Cast on 42 (46, 48) sts.

Rows 1 through 33: Work even in garter st.

Row 34, wrong side: Inc 1 st at each side by k in front and back of the 1st and the last st.

Rows 35 through 52: Work even in garter st over 44 (48, 50) sts.

Shape Underarm:

Rows 53 and 54: K and bind off the 1st 3 (3,3) sts of each row.

Rows 55 and 56: Sl 1, k 1, psso at the beg of each row to dec 1 st.

Rows 57 through 93: Work even in garter st over the rem 36 (40, 42) sts.

Row 94, wrong side: K and bind off all sts.

RIGHT FRONT:

Cast on 3 sts.

Shape Point: Right side: K 3. Wrong side: Cast on 4 sts by knit-on method, * k 1, pull up loop, place on left-hand needle and tighten, rep from * until there are 7 sts on left-hand needle, then k 6, k 1-inc 1, turn, k 8 on right side, turn, cast on 4 sts, then k 11, k 1-inc 1, turn, k 13, turn, cast on 4 sts, then k 16, k 1-inc 1, turn, k 18, turn, cast on 4 sts, then k 21, k 1-inc 1, turn, k 23, turn, cast on 1 (3, 4) then k 23 (25, 26), k 1-inc 1, turn, k 25 (27, 28), turn, cast on 1 (1, 2), then k 25 (27, 29), k 1-inc 1, turn.

Row 1 (at same level as Row 1 on back), right side: K 27 (29,31).

Rows 2, 3, and 4: Rep Row 1.

Row 5, bind off for buttonhole: K 4, then pass 3rd st over 4th st just knitted, k 23 (25, 27).

Row 6, cast on for buttonhole: K 24 (26, 28), turn to right side, k 1 in st on left-hand needle, pull up loop and place on same needle, turn, and k 2.

Rows 7 through 12 (6 rows): Work even.

Rows 13 through 44: Rep Rows 5 through 12 four times and inc 1 st at side on Row 34.

Rows 45 and 46: Make the 6th buttonhole as on Rows 5 and 6.

Rows 47 and 48: K 28 (30, 32).

Begin Neck Shaping:

Row 49, right side: K and bind off the first 5 sts, k 23 (25, 27).

Row 50: Work even.

Row 51: Bind off the first 2 sts (sl 1, k 1, psso, k 1, psso), k to end of row.

Row 52: K 21 (23, 25).

Row 53: Rep Row 51.

Shape Underarm:

Row 54, wrong side: K and bind off first 4 (4, 5) sts, k 15 (17, 17).

Row 55: Rep Row 51.

Rows 56, 57, and 58: Bind off 1 st at beg of each row.

Rows 59 through 95: Work even at the armhole edge. Bind off 1 st at neckline edge two (three, three) times more, then work even over rem 8 (9, 9) sts.

Row 96, wrong side: K and bind off.

LEFT FRONT:

Work as right front, reversing shapings.

To Assemble: Count 8 (9, 9) sts for each back shoulder and sew to each front strap. Sew side seams edge to edge without seam allowance, matching ridges in pattern carefully.

Blue Linen Lace Pullover

Sizes and Measurements:

Chest: Sizes 6 and 8 measure 34″ (17″ across the back or front).
Sizes 10 (12, 14) measure 42″ (21″ across the back or front).
Hip band: Size 6 = 32″, size 8 = 34″, sizes 10 to 12 = 36″, and size 14 = 38″.
The length from shoulder to lower edge measures 27″ in all sizes.
The sleeve length is 18½″.

Materials:

Size 5/2 linen yarn: 1½ lbs. to make sizes 6 and 8, 2 lbs. to make sizes 10 (12, 14).

Needles:

Size 8, or size to obtain gauge.

Gauge:

Lace Pattern: 24 sts (1 pattern repeat) = 4¼″, 16 rows (4 pattern repeats) = 3″.

Lace Pattern:

Rows 1 and 3, right side: K all sts.
Row 2, wrong side: P all sts.
Row 4, wrong side: K 2 tog four times, * (yo, k 1) eight times, k 2 tog eight times, rep from *, end (yo, k 1) eight times, k 2 tog four times.

BACK:

Directions for sizes 10 (12, 14) are shown within parentheses.
Cast on 52 sts for size 6, 56 sts for size 8, 60 sts for sizes 10 to 12, and 64 sts for size 14.
Rows 1 through 23: Work even in garter st.
Row 24, inc to 96 (120) sts on wrong side:
Size 6, k 4, k in front and back of each of the next 44 sts, k 4.
Size 8, k 8, k in front and back of each of the next 40 sts, k 8.
Sizes 10 and 12, k in front and back of every st.
Size 14, k 4, k in front and back of each of 56 sts, k 4.

Begin Lace Pattern:

Rows 25 through 139: Rep Rows 1 through 4 twenty-eight times, then work Rows 1, 2, and 3 again. Every Row 4 rep from * three (four) times.

Row 140, dec to 64 (80) sts on wrong side: K 2 tog four times, * k 8, k 2 tog eight times, rep from * three (four) times, k 8, k 2 tog four times.

Rows 141 through 149: Work even in garter st.

Row 150, wrong side: K and bind off all sts at the same time.

FRONT:

Make exactly the same as the back.

SLEEVE:

Cast on 30 sts for sizes 6 and 8 and 36 sts for sizes 10 (12, 14).

Rows 1 through 23: Work even in garter st.

Row 24, inc to 60 (72) sts on wrong side: K in front and back of every st.

Begin Lace Pattern: Sizes 6 and 8 only, inc to 72 sts over the 1st 3 rows in lace pattern. Inc 2 sts at the beg and at end of each row (k or p in the row below 1st and last 2 sts three times).

Sizes 10 (12, 14): Work Rows 1, 2, and 3 of lace pattern (Rows 25, 26, 27).

Row 28, Row 4 in lace pattern: Rep from * twice.

Rows 29 through 91: Rep Rows 1 through 4 in lace pattern fifteen times, then work Rows 1, 2, and 3 again.

Row 92, wrong side: K 72 sts.

Rows 93 through 101:

Sizes 6 and 8: Work in garter st and dec 1 st at the beg and end of every 2nd row three times, then work even over 66 sts.

Sizes 10 and 12: Work even in garter st.

Size 14: Work in garter st and inc 1 st at the beg and end of every 2nd row three times, then work even over 78 sts.

Row 102, wrong side: K and bind off all sts.

To Assemble: Leave 8″ (10″) opening for neck at top edge and sew shoulders. Leave 7½″ for sizes 6 and 8, 8½″ for sizes 10 and 12, and 9½″ for size 14 opened for armholes and sew side seams. Seam sleeves and set into armholes. Steam-press sweater.

White and Green
Blouson with Flowers

Sizes and Measurements:

Chest: The finished sweater measures 37″ for sizes 8 and 10, 40″ for sizes 12 and 14, and 44″ for sizes 16 and 18.
The sleeve measures 15″ (16½″, 16½″) around.
The length of the body from lower edge to underarm is 14″ in all sizes.
The length of the sleeve to underarm is 18½″ in all sizes.

Materials:

Sports yarn: 6 (7, 7) oz. each of White and Green and ¼ oz. each of Lavender, Blue, and Pink.

1 Knitting spool to make ties (or 1 crochet hook size H).

Needles:

Size 5—1 pair 10″ and 1 circular 36″.

Gauge:

Stockinette stitch: 6 sts = 1″, 8 rows = 1″.

BACK:

With Green, cast on 113 (123, 133) sts.
Row 1, right side: K all sts.
Row 2: P all sts.
Rows 3 through 14: Rep Rows 1 and 2.

Begin Flower Pattern:
Row 15, right side: With Green, k all sts.
Row 16: With Green, k 5, * k 3 wrapping yarn around the needle three times for each st, k 7, rep from * ten (eleven, twelve) times, end k 3 wrapping yarn three times for each st, k5.
Row 17: With White, k 1, sl 1 with yarn in back, * k 3, sl 3 with yarn in back, dropping extra length in loop, k 3, sl 1 with yarn in back, rep from * ten (eleven, twelve) times, end k 1.
Row 18: With White, p 1, sl 1 with yarn in front, * p 3, sl 3 with yarn in front, p 3, sl with yarn in front, rep from * ten (eleven, twelve) times, end p 1.

Row 19: With White, k 5, * sl 3 with yarn in back, k 7, rep from * ten (eleven, twelve) times, end sl 3 with yarn in back, k 5.

Row 20: With White, p 5, * sl 3 with yarn in front, p 7, rep from * ten (eleven, twelve, thirteen) times, end sl 3 with yarn in front, p 5.

Row 21: With White, k 3, * sl 2 with yarn in back, drop 1st Green st off the needle to front of work, sl same 2 sts back on left-hand needle, pick up dropped st and knit it, k 2, k the 2nd Green st, drop the 3rd Green st to front of work, k 2, pick up the dropped st and knit it, k 3, rep from * ten (eleven, twelve) times.

Row 22: With Pink, sl 3 with yarn in front, * (p 1, k 1, p 1 in next st, sl 2 with yarn in front) twice, p 1, k 1, p 1 in next st, sl 3 with yarn in front, rep from * ten (eleven, twelve) times.

Row 23: With Pink, sl 3 with yarn in back, * (p 3, turn, k 3, turn, sl 1, k 2 tog, psso, sl 2 with yarn in back) twice, p 3, turn, k 3, turn, sl 1, k 2 tog, psso, sl 3 with yarn in back, rep from * ten (eleven, twelve) times.

Row 24: With White, p, but work each Pink st *in the back.*

Rows 25 through 32 (8 rows): With White, work st st.

Rows 33 through 50 (18 rows): Rep Rows 15 through 32, but work Rows 22 and 23 with Blue.

Rows 51 through 68 (18 rows): Rep Rows 15 through 32, but work Rows 22 and 23 with Lavender.

Rows 69 through 122 (54 rows): Rep Rows 15 through 68.

Rows 123 through 132 (10 rows): Rep Rows 15 through 24.

Rows 133 and 134: With White, work even in st st.

Shape Underarm: Continue with White and st st.

Rows 135 and 136: Bind off the 1st 6 sts of each row.

Rows 137 through 140 (4 rows): Bind off 5 sts at the beg of each row. Place rem 81 (91, 101) sts on a holder.

THE FRONT:

Make exactly the same as the back.

SLEEVE:

With Green, cast on 93 (103, 103) sts.

Rows 1 through 14: With Green, work in st st.

Rows 15 through 176 (162 rows): Rep Rows 15 through 68 of back three times, working 9 (10, 10) groups of flowers across.

Rows 177 through 186 (10 rows): Rep Rows 15 through 24 of back.

Rows 187 and 188: With White, work in st st.

Shape Underarm:

Rows 189 through 194: Rep Rows 135 through 140 of back. Place rem 61 (71, 71) sts on a holder.

YOKE:

Turn all the pieces to the right side and place the sts from holders onto the circular needle, beg at center front. Sl 40 (45, 50) sts of right front onto needle, then s1 61 (71, 71) sts from right sleeve, 81 (91, 101) sts from back, 61 (71, 71) sts from left sleeve, and then place rem 41 (46, 51) sts at left front onto the needle.

Row 1, right side of sweater: With Green, k 284 (324, 344) sts.

Rows 2 through 36: Continue with Green and k back and forth on the circular needle, turning every row at center front until 18 garter st ridges are completed.

Row 37, work *short rows*, making the back longer than the front: K 264 (304, 324), turn, leaving 20 sts at end, sl 1, k 243 (283, 303), turn, leaving 20 sts at end, sl 1, k 223 (263, 283), turn, leaving 40 sts at end, sl 1, k 203 (243, 263), turn, leaving 40 sts at end, sl 1, k 183 (223, 243), turn, leaving 60 sts at end, k 163 (203, 223), turn, leaving 60 sts at end, sl 1, k 143 (183, 203), turn, leaving 80 sts at end, sl 1, k 123 (163, 183), turn, leaving 80 sts at end, sl 1, k 103 (143, 163), turn, leaving 100 sts at end, sl 1, k 83 (123, 143), turn, leaving 100 sts at end, sl 1, k 63 (103, 123), turn, leaving 120 sts at end, sl 1, k 43 (83, 103), turn, leaving 120 sts at end, sl 1, k to center left front—163 (203, 223) sts.

Row 38, wrong side: K from center left front to center right front 284 (324, 344) sts.

Row 39, right side: Dec to 142 (162, 172) sts, k 2 tog across the row.

Rows 40 through 44: Work even in garter st over 142 (162, 172) sts. (22 garter st ridges at center front and 28 ridges at center back completed.)

Change to Stockinette Stitch:

Rows 45 through 58: K on the right side and p on the wrong side.

Row 59, right side: K and bind off all sts loosely.

TIES:

Make ties on the knitting spool with Green. Complete 24″ for each sleeve, 38″ (42″, 46″) for the neck and 38″ (42″, 46″) for lower edge of sweater.

To Crochet Ties: With hook size H and double strand of Green, ch st to measure the same as above, turn, sk 1 ch, then sl st back in every ch st.

To Assemble: Sew side seams and sleeves edge to edge without seam allowances. Match bound-off stitches at underarms and sew together. Roll stockinette stitch bands forward and sew the 10th purl row to the first garter stitch row immediately following the stockinette stitch rows. Leave small openings at center of each sleeve and at center lower edge of front. Thread the knitted (crocheted) ties through the rolled edges. Knot each end of ties, then pull to gather fullness in sweater and tie.

White and Gray Double-Breasted Coat with Shawl Collar

Sizes and Coat Measurements:

The length of the coat is 47″ from the shoulder to the lower edge.
To adjust the length, work longer or shorter before pocket.
The sleeve measures 18½″ from underarm to lower edge. Adjust the length, if necessary, before the first increase.

Chest measurements:

Small (8 to 10), 37″, Medium (12 to 14), 43″, and Large (16 to 18), 49″. Directions for Medium and Large are shown in parentheses.

Materials:

Heavy knitting worsted, 28 (32, 36) oz. of White and 16 (20, 20) oz. of Light Gray.

4 Buttons, each measuring 1¼″ in diameter.

Needles:

Size 9, or size to obtain gauge.

Gauge:

Garter stitch: 4 sts = 1″.
Slip stitch pattern: 5 sts = 1″.
Garter stitch and slip stitch pattern: 8 rows = 1″.

BACK:

The back is made in an even rectangle to measure 17″ (20″, 23″) across by 47″ to shoulder. (When shaping shoulders 1″ is added to length at back neck.)
With White, cast on 85 (101, 117) sts.
Rows 1 through 7: Work in garter st with White.
Row 8, wrong side: P with White.
Begin slip stitch pattern with 2 colors.

Row 9, right side: With Gray, sl 2 with yarn in front. k 1, * sl 3 with yarn in front, k 1, rep from *, end sl 2 with yarn in front.

Row 10: With Gray, p all sts.

Row 11, right side: With White, k 1, * sl 3 with yarn in front, k 1, rep from *.

Row 12: With White p all sts.

Rows 13 through 337: Rep Rows 9 through 12 eighty-one times; then work Row 9 once more. When changing to Gray throw White yarn *forward* and sl Gray behind. When changing color again, the Gray slip thread will then be pulled up at the edge.

Shape Shoulders:

Row 338, wrong side: With Gray, p and bind off the first 16 (20, 24) sts, p 53 (61, 69), p and bind off 16 (20, 24) sts. Cut thread.

Row 339, right side: With White, work as Row 11 over 53 (61, 69) sts.

Row 340: With White, p and bind off the first 16 (20, 24) sts, p 21, p and bind off the last 16 (20, 24) sts.

Row 341: With Gray, work as Row 9 over rem 21 sts.

Row 342: With Gray, p and bind off 21 sts.

RIGHT FRONT:

Each front measures 13″ (14½″, 16″) across (or 7″ (8½″, 10″) of sl st pattern plus 6″ of overlapping White border.

With White, cast on 58 (66, 74) sts.

Rows 1 through 7: K in garter st with White.

Row 8, wrong side: P with White.

Begin slip stitch pattern and White front border.

Row 9, right side: With White, k 25; with Gray, sl 2 with yarn in front, k 1, * sl 3 with yarn in front, k 1, rep from *, end sl 2 with yarn in front.

Row 10: With Gray, p 33 (41, 49): with White, k 25.

Row 11, right side: With White, k 25, * k 1, sl 3 with yarn in front, rep from *, end k 1.

Row 12: With White, p 33 (41, 49), k 25.

Rows 13 through 160: Rep Rows 9 through 12 thirty-seven times but *skip* 2 rows (1 garter st ridge) at front border every 4th rep of pattern eight times. (This will eliminate 16 rows or 8 ridges from front border between lower edge and first buttonholes and will prevent front edge from sagging.) Twist White and Gray yarns on the wrong side when changing colors to avoid holes. Work all rows on front border hereafter.

Row 161: Rep Row 9.

Row 162, wrong side: With Gray, p 33 (41, 49), then work front

border and bind off for buttonholes. With White, k 5, k and bind off the next 3 sts, k 9, k and bind off 3 sts, k 5.

Row 163, right side: Cast on for buttonholes. With White, k 5, turn to the wrong side of work, * k 1 in 1st st on left-hand needle, pull up loop and place on same needle, tighten st, rep from * twice more (3 sts), turn work to the right side and k 9, turn to wrong side and rep from *, turn to right side and k 5, then work sl st pattern as Row 11 over 33 (41, 49) sts.

Row 164: Rep Row 12.

Rows 165 through 200: Rep Rows 9 through 12 nine times.

Row 201: Rep Row 9.

Make pocket opening and 2nd pair of buttonholes.

Row 202, wrong side: With Gray, p 5 (9, 13), then place the next 23 sts on holder. Turn to right side of work, * k 1 in 1st st on left hand needle, pull up loop and place on the same needle, rep from * until 23 sts have been cast on, turn to wrong side of work and p 5 (9, 13). With White, k 5, k and bind off the next 3 sts, k 9, k and bind off 3 sts, k 5.

Row 203: Rep Row 163, casting on for buttonholes.

Row 204: Rep Row 12.

Rows 205 through 336: Rep Rows 9 through 12 thirty-three times.

Inc for Collar on 83rd Pattern Repeat:

Row 337: Rep Row 9.

Row 338, wrong side: With Gray, p 33 (41, 49). With White, k in front and back of 1st border st, k 24.

Row 339: With White, k 26, * k 1, sl 3 with yarn in front, rep from *, end k 1.

Shape Shoulder and Inc Collar:

Row 340, wrong side: With White, p and bind off 16 (20, 24), p 17 (21, 25), k in front and back of 1st border st, k 25.

Row 341: With White, k 27. With Gray, sl 2 with yarn in front, k 1, * sl 3 with yarn in front, k 1, rep from * end sl 2 with yarn in front.

Row 342: With Gray, p and bind off 16 (20, 24). With White, k in front and back of 1st st of border, k 26.

Collar:

Row 343, right side: With White k 29.

Row 344: K in front and back of 1st st, k 28.

Rows 345 through 367 (23 rows): K in garter st with White over 30 sts.

Row 368, right side of turned-over collar: K and bind off 30 sts.

LEFT FRONT:

With White, cast on 58 (66, 74) sts; then work Rows 1 through 8 as on right front.

Row 9, right side: With Gray, sl 2 with yarn in front, k 1, * sl 3 with yarn in front, k 1, rep from * seven (nine, eleven) times, sl 2 with yarn in front, 33 (41, 49) sts, turn.

Row 10: With Gray, p 33 (41, 49) sts.

Row 11, right side: With White, k 1, * sl 3 with yarn in front, k 1, rep from * eight (ten, twelve) times, k 25.

Work missing rows on border sts only;

Row 9: With White, k 25, turn,

Row 10: With White, k 25.

Row 12: With White, k 25, p 33 (41, 49).

Rows 13 through 200: Rep Rows 9 through 12 forty-eight times. Skip Rows 9 and 10 on every 4th rep eight times.

Row 201: Rep Row 9.

Row 202: Make pocket opening as on right front.

Rows 203 and 204: Rep Rows 11 and 12.

Rows 205 through 368: Work as for right front, inc the collar and bind off for shoulder on same numbered rows.

SLEEVE:

With White, cast on 65 (65, 73) sts and work Rows 1 through 8 as for back.

Rows 9 through 64: Work sl st pattern as for back, rep Rows 9 through 12 fourteen times.

Row 65: Rep Row 9.

Row 66: Inc 1 st at each side. With Gray, p 1, p 1 in the row below, p to the last st, p 1 in the row below, p the last st.

Row 67, right side: With White, sl 1 with yarn in front, k 1, * sl 3 with yarn in front, k 1, rep from *, end sl 1 with yarn in front.

Rows 68 and 70: Rep Rows 10 and 12 of back.

Row 69, right side: With Gray, sl 3, * k 1, sl 3, rep from *.

Rows 71 through 85: Rep Rows 67 through 70 three times, then work Rows 67, 68, and 69 again (15 rows).

Row 86: Inc 1 st at each side as on Row 66.

Row 87, right side: With White, sl 2, k 1, * sl 3, k 1, rep from *, end sl 2.

Rows 88 and 90: Rep Rows 10 and 12 of back.

Row 89: With Gray, k 1, * sl 3, k 1, rep from *.

Rows 91 through 105: Rep Rows 87 through 90 three times, then work Rows 87, 88, and 89 again.

Row 106: Inc 1 st at each side as on Row 66.

Row 107, right side: With White, sl 3, * k 1, sl 3, rep from *.

Rows 108 and 110: Rep Rows 10 and 12 of back.

Row 109, right side: With Gray, sl 1, k 1, * sl 3, k 1, rep from *, end sl 1.

Rows 111 through 125: Rep Rows 107 through 110 three times, then work Rows 107, 108, and 109 again.

Row 126: Inc 1 st at each side as on Row 66.

Row 127, right side: With White, k 1, * sl 3, k 1, rep from *.

Rows 128 and 130: p 73 (73, 81).

Row 129, right side: With Gray, sl 2, k 1, * sl 3, k 1, rep from *, end sl 2.

Rows 131 through 141: Rep Rows 127 through 130 twice, then work Rows 127, 128, 129 again (11 rows). Cut White and Gray threads.

Work White border at armhole.

Row 142, wrong side: With White, k 73 (73, 81).

Rows 143 through 148: Rep Row 142 (4 garter st ridges).

Row 147, right side: K and bind off all sts.

POCKET:

White border: On the right side of knit, place 25 sts on needle from right to left along lower edge of opening. Pick up 1 st at right edge, sl 23 from holder onto needle, pick up 1 st at left edge.

Row 1, wrong side: K 25 with White.

Rows 2 through 6: K in garter st.

Row 7, wrong side: K and bind off.

Inside Pocket: On the wrong side of knit, pick up 25 sts along the upper edge of opening.

Rows 1 through 30: With Gray, work in st st. Bind off.

To Assemble: Block all pieces, sew fronts to back shoulders and seam collar together at center back. Measure 8½″ (8½″, 9″) from shoulder down each front and back and mark for underarms. From markers seam together sides of coat, carefully matching running threads in sl st pattern. Sew sleeves and set into body armholes. Press pocket flat, pin down in a straight line on the wrong side and sew around the edges. Attach the edges of White pocket borders in even lines. Sew on button at same level as each buttonhole.

Diamond-Patterned
Mohair Pullover
in Nine Colors

Sizes and Measurements:

Chest: Sizes 8 (10, 12) measure 18″ and 30″ from shoulder to lower edge of ribbing. Sizes 14 (16, 18) measure 22½″ and 30″ from shoulder to lower edge.

The sleeve length for both sizes is 18½″ from underarm to lower edge of cuff.

Directions for sizes 14 to 18 are shown in parentheses.

Materials:

16 40-gr. Balls of mohair: 4 Turquoise; 2 each of Green, Orange, Blue, and Cranberry; 1 each of Red, Purple, Rust, and Coral.

Needles:

Size 10, or size to obtain gauge.

Gauge:

Garter stitch: 3 sts = 1″, 6 rows = 1″.

Each bias-knitted square 10 sts × 20 rows should measure 3¼″ × 3¼″ and 4½″ between opposite corners.

Note: The front and back of the sweater are knitted exactly the same, beginning with ribbing at lower edge. At underarm the stitches for the sleeves are cast on and knitted together with the body to the shoulder. The stitches for cuffs and high neck are picked up along edges of the finished body and worked in ribbing.

BACK:

With Turquoise, cast on 52 (64) sts.

Row 1, right side: P 1, * k 2, p 2, rep from * twelve (fifteen) times, k 2, p 1.

Row 2: K 1, * p 2, k 2, rep from * twelve (fifteen) times, p 2, k 1.

Rows 3 through 23: Rep Rows 1 and 2 ten times, then rep Row 2 once more.

Row 24, dec to 40 (50) sts: K 2 (k 4), * k 2 tog, k 2, rep from * twelve (fourteen) times, k 2 (k 4).

Begin body pattern by making 4 (5) triangles with Turquoise yarn: * K 2 on right side of sweater, turn, k 2 on wrong side, turn, k 3, turn, k 3, turn, k 4, turn, k 4, turn, k 5, turn, k 5, turn, k 6, turn, k 6, turn, k 7, turn, k 7, turn, k 8, turn, k 8, turn, k 9, turn, k 9, turn, k 10, turn, k 10, turn, k 10 on right side. The 1st triangle is completed. Keep the sts on the left-hand needle while working the other triangles or place the sts of each finished triangle on separate holders. Rep from * to make 2nd, 3rd, and 4th (and 5th) triangles.

First row of squares: Make 3 (4) full squares and 1 half-square at each side of sweater. Begin at the last completed triangle and make 1 half-square. With Red, p 2 on wrong side of sweater, turn, k 2 on right side, turn, k 1-inc 1, sl 1, p 1, psso, turn, k 3, turn, k 1-inc 1, k 1, sl 1 p 1, psso, turn, k 4, turn, k 1-inc 1, k 2, sl 1, p 1, psso, turn, k 5, turn, k 1-inc 1, k 3, sl 1, p 1, psso, turn, k 6, turn, k 1-inc 1, k 4, sl 1, p 1, psso, turn, k 7, turn, k 1-inc 1, k 5, sl 1, p 1, psso, turn, k 8, turn, k 1-inc 1, k 6, sl 1, p 1, psso, turn, k 9, turn, k 1-inc 1, k 7, sl 1, p 1, psso, turn, k 10, turn, k 10 on wrong side. Half-square completed. Keep sts on needle or move to holder.

Continue first row of squares and make one full square: ** Turn to right side of sweater and with the needle holding all unworked sts pick up 10 sts along the right edge of base triangle (insert the needle into the last st of each of 10 garter st ridges in triangle), turn to wrong side of sweater and with Red p 10, turn, * k 10 on right side, turn to wrong side and k 9, k the last st tog with the 1st st of next triangle, rep from * nine times more to complete square. All the sts from triangle should be knitted into square and there should be 10 garter st ridges (20 rows) in square. Keep sts on needle or place on holder. Rep from ** to make 2nd, 3rd (and 4th) squares, then make 1 half-square at side of sweater: Turn to right side of sweater. With the empty needle pick up 10 sts along the right edge of rem base triangle, turn to wrong side and p 10, turn, k 10, turn, k 8, k 2 tog, turn, k 9, turn, k 7, k 2 tog, turn, k 8, turn, k 6, k 2 tog, turn, k 7, turn, k 5, k 2 tog, turn, k 6, turn, k 4, k 2 tog, turn, k 5, turn, k 3, k 2 tog, turn, k 4, turn, k 2, k 2 tog, turn, k 3, turn, k 1, k 2 tog, turn, k 2, turn, k 2 tog, turn, k 1. Hold the last st for next row.

Second row of squares: Make 4 (5) full squares. Turn to wrong side of sweater and with the needle holding all unworked sts

pick up 9 sts along the edge of just-completed half-square, then place the last st onto the same needle. Turn to right side and with Purple, ** k 10, turn, * k 10 on wrong side, turn, k 9, sl 1, k 1 from the next square, psso, turn, rep from * nine times more to complete 1st square. Turn to wrong side and pick up 10 sts along the edge of Red square, then turn to right side and rep from ** for 2nd square. Rep from ** twice (three times) more.

Third row of squares: Rep 1st row of squares with Rust.

Fourth row of squares: Rep 2nd row of squares with Turquoise.

Fifth row of squares: Rep 1st row of squares with Coral.

Sixth row of squares: Rep 2nd row of squares with Green.
Place all sts of body onto holder and begin sleeves.

LEFT SLEEVE:

With Green, cast on 30 sts loosely, then work 3 triangles in same way as the 1st base triangles were made at the beginning of sweater. When the triangles are completed, rep first row of squares with Orange, making 1 half-square at edge and then 2 full squares. With the empty needle pick up 10 sts along right edge of the 3rd base triangle, turn to the wrong side and p 10 with Orange, turn, k 10, turn, k 9 on wrong side, then hold the last st, place all the sts of body onto empty needle, then k the last st of sleeve tog with the 1st st of body. Cont as before, completing the 3rd square. Then rep pattern making 3 (4) squares across the body. Hold the sts and begin right sleeve.

RIGHT SLEEVE:

With Green, cast on 30 sts and work 3 triangles. Then with the same needle holding base triangles, pick up 10 sts along the edge of Green square not yet worked on body. Turn to wrong side of sweater and p 10 with Orange, turn, k 10, turn, k 9 then k the last st of body tog with the 1st st of sleeve. Cont as before, completing the 7th (8th) square, then work 2 more squares and 1 half-square at the end of right sleeve.
The 7th row of squares is now completed with Orange and the sleeves are attached to the body. Work now from one end of sleeve to the opposite end.

Eighth row of squares: Rep 2nd row of squares with Blue, completing 10 (11) squares.

Ninth row of squares: Rep 1st row of squares with Cranberry.

Tenth row: With Turquoise, work one row of triangles to fill in spaces between each square. Turn to wrong side of sweater and pick up 9 sts along the edge of the just-completed half-square, then place the last st of half-square onto same needle. Turn to right side and k 10, turn, k 10, turn, * k 9, sl 1, k 1, psso on right side, turn, k 8, k 2 tog on wrong side, turn, k 8, sl 1, k 1, psso, turn, k 7, k 2 tog, turn, k 7, sl 1, k 1, psso, turn, k 6, k 2 tog, turn, k 6, sl 1, k 1, psso, turn, k 5, k 2 tog, turn, k 5, sl 1, k 1, psso, turn, k 4, k 2 tog, turn, k 4, sl 1, k 1, psso, turn, k 3, k 2 tog, turn, k 3, sl 1, k 1, psso, turn, k 2, k 2 tog, turn, k 2, sl 1, k 1, psso, turn, k 1, k 2 tog, turn, k 1, sl 1, k 1, psso, turn, k 2 tog, turn, sl 1, k 1, psso. Keep the last st on needle.
** Turn to wrong side of sweater and pick up 10 sts along the edge of next square, turn to right side and k 10 onto same needle, holding leftover st from previous triangle, turn, k 9, k 2 tog, turn, then rep from * to complete 2nd triangle.
For the 3rd through 10th (11th) triangles: Rep from **.

FRONT:

Make exactly as the back.

HIGH NECK:

Sizes 8 (10, 12): Pick up 15 sts along the edge of the 5th and 6th triangles at top of sweater center front, then pick up 15 sts along the edge of the 5th and 6th triangles at center back (60 sts).
Sizes 14 (16, 18): Count 4½ triangles along top edge of sweater from end of sleeves toward center back and front. Mark neck opening to be half of 5th triangle, 6th triangle, and half of 7th triangle. Pick up 15 sts along the edge of front, then 15 sts along edge of back neck (60 sts).
Both sizes:
Row 1, wrong side: K 1, * p 2, k 2, rep from *, end p 2, k 1.
Row 2: P 1, * k 2, p 2, rep from *, end k 2, p 1.
Rows 3 through 40: Rep Rows 1 and 2 nineteen times. Bind off.

SLEEVE CUFF:

Pick up 19 sts along wrong side edge of each front and back sleeve (38 sts).

Row 1, right side: Dec to 28 sts, * k 2 tog, k 2, rep from * nine
   times, k 2 tog.
Row 2: K 1, * p 2, k 2, rep from *, end p 2, k 1.
Row 3: P 1, * k 2, p 2, rep from *, end k 2, p 1.
Rows 4 through 19: Rep Rows 2 and 3 eight times.
Row 20: Rep Row 2 and bind off at the same time.

To Assemble: Seam all ribbed parts of sweater—cuffs, high
neck, and back to front body ribbing. Sew back to front,
matching triangles carefully at all edges and using same color
yarn as in each triangle.

Barbara Baker

In addition to her professional knitting career, Barbara, in association with her writer-filmmaker husband, has worked extensively in costume, set, and lighting design for many live theater productions. In motion pictures she has worked as a script supervisor, researcher, writer, and editor. She co-wrote and co-directed three films with her husband, including the documentary Lenny Bruce Without Tears. A serious craftswoman since childhood, Barbara has always been fascinated with the art of knitting and experimenting with texture and color in fashion design. She designs primarily for yarn companies, including Spinnerin, Coats & Clark, Columbia-Minerva, and Reynolds. Her work has also appeared in Good Housekeeping, and her designs in that magazine have won a lot of people's seal of approval.

"I rarely just pick up a new yarn and begin knitting a specific piece. I want to know more about the yarn and what it can do before I put it into a garment. I'll experiment with it to see how it looks worked in different stitches and how it combines with other yarns. It isn't until I really know the yarn that I start to design.

"Fit is very important to me and I work very hard on the fit and flow of a garment. But if a knitted garment doesn't exactly fit the person you made it for, you can avoid heavy blocking by putting the garment on its owner and then working it into the proper shape using the wearer as a guide. That's what's so fabulous about knitting; the material gives and moves and takes the form of the person it is made for. Knitting is very flexible, and the only thing that can remove that flexibility is blocking with an iron. I almost always wet-block my garments. I soak the work and squeeze out the excess moisture. Then I lay the knitting on a towel, form it to the measurements I want, and let it dry. This does marvelous things to the knitting. I recently wet-blocked a cable knit; it made the cables open up beautifully and evened out all the stitches. I recommend it for just about every kind of knitting."

Barbara Baker

Woman's Chenille Jacket

Sizes:

Directions are for Small. Changes for Medium and Large are in parentheses.

Size Equivalents:

Woman's Small size fits 32" bust; Medium size fits 34"; Large size fits 36".
Man's Small size fits 38" chest; Medium size fits 40"; Large size fits 42".

Materials:

Rayon chenille sport-weight yarn: 2¼ lbs. (2½ lbs., 2¾ lbs).

Tapestry needle.

Size J crochet hook.

Entire sweater is worked with 2 strands of chenille yarn.

Needles:

Size 8, or size to obtain gauge.

Gauge:

3½ sts = 1", 5 rows = 1".

Pattern Stitch:

Row 1, right side: K across.
Row 2: P across.
Row 3: K across.
Row 4: * K 1, with yarn in back of needle sl 1. Rep from * across.

BACK:

Cast on 59 (63, 67) sts. Work in patt st for 15 (15½", 16"). Mark with contrasting yarn for armholes. Cont in patt st until entire piece measures 23" (23¾", 24½").

Shoulder Shaping: Bind off 6 (7, 7) sts at beg of next 4 rows. Then bind off 6 (6, 7) sts at beg of next 2 rows. Bind off rem 23 (23, 25) sts for neck.

RIGHT FRONT:

Cast on 45 (49, 53) sts. Work in patt st for 5″ (5½″, 6″). On right side, dec 1 st at front edge every 4 rows, or after each ridge row, twenty-seven, twenty-nine, thirty-two times. Work on rem 18 (20, 21) sts until front measures 23″ (23¾″, 24½″).

Shoulder Shaping: At right shoulder edge, bind off 6 (7, 7) sts every other row twice, then 6 (6, 7) sts once.

LEFT FRONT:

Work to correspond to right front, being sure to reverse all shapings.

SLEEVES:

Cast on 59 (61, 63) sts. Work in garter st for 4″. Change to patt st and work for 14″. Dec 1 st at beg and end of row. Cont in patt st until sleeve measures about 22″ (22½″, 23″). Bind off. Sew right shoulder seam.

Crochet Front Edge: With 3 strands of chenille and size J crochet hook, starting at lower right front edge, sc in every 3rd row, up right front edge, across neck and down left front edge.

Finishing: Sew left shoulder and sleeve seams. Leaving top 8″ (8¼″, 8½″) open for armholes, sew side seams. Sew top edge of sleeves to armholes. Turn a 4″ cuff to right side at lower edge of sleeve.

BELT:

Cast on 5 sts. Work in k 1, p 1, ribbing until length measures 52″ (54″, 56″), or desired length. Knot belt at each end.

Man's Alpaca
V-Neck Pullover

Size:

Directions are for Small. Changes for Medium and Large are in parentheses.

Materials:

Alpaca yarn: 12 oz. (13 oz., 14 oz.) White, 12 oz. (13 oz., 14 oz.) Brown, 2 oz. (2 oz., 2 oz.) Black.

Tapestry needle.

Needles:

Sizes 5 and 7, or sizes to obtain gauge.

Gauge:

4½–5 sts = 1″, 6 rows = 1″.

BACK:

With size 5 needles and Brown, cast on 88 (93, 98) sts. Work k 2, p 2 ribbing for 3″, inc 4 (5,4) sts evenly spaced across last row—92 (98, 102) sts. Change to size 7 needles and work 2 rows in st st. Att White and work 2 rows st st. Det White and with Brown cont working in st st for 8″ (8½″, 9″). Att White and work 2 rows White, 2 rows Brown, 2 rows White. Att Black. Work design in Black, following the chart. Att Brown. Work 2 rows Brown, 2 rows White, 2 rows Brown, 2 rows White, 2 rows Brown. Det Brown.

Armhole Shaping: With White, bind off 5 sts at beg of next 2 rows. On next row dec 1 st at each side every other row as follows:

Row 1, right side: K 3, k 2 tog, k across to last 5 sts, k 2 tog, k 3.
Row 2: P. Rep these 2 rows four times more for full-fashioned shaping—72 (78, 82) sts. Cont in st st until armhole measures 9″ (9½″, 10″).

Shoulder Shaping: Bind off 5 (6, 6) sts at beg of next 4 rows, then 5 (5, 6) sts at beg of next 4 rows. Place rem 32 (34, 36) sts on holder.

FRONT:

With size 5 needles and Brown, cast on 88 (93, 98) sts. Work k 2, p 2 ribbing for 3″, inc 3 (4, 3) sts evenly spaced across last row—91 (97, 101) sts. Work same as back to armholes.

Armhole and V-Neck Shaping: At arm edge, bind off 5 sts at beg of next 2 rows. Dec 1 st at arm edge every other row five times in same manner as back—81 (87, 91) sts. At same time divide for V-neck. On right side, k across 40 (43, 45) sts. Place center st on safety pin. Join second ball of yarn, k across 40 (43, 45) sts. P back. Cont working full-fashioned decs at arm edge and neck edge in same manner as back. At neck edge, dec 1 st every 3rd row fifteen (sixteen, sixteen) times. Work in st st on rem 20 (22, 24) sts until armhole measures same as back. Shape shoulders as for back.

SLEEVES:

With size 5 needles and Brown, cast on 44 (48, 52) sts. Work in k 2, p 2 ribbing for 3″, inc 1 st at each end of last row. Change to size 7 needles and work 2 rows in st st. Att White and work 2 rows White. Det White. Work Brown in st st for 4 more rows. Inc 1 st at each end, then inc 2 sts at each end every 8 rows ten times more—68 (72, 76) sts. At same time, when sleeve measures 15″ (15½″, 16″), work White and Brown stripes, then follow color chart ending with Brown and White stripes in same manner as body of sweater.

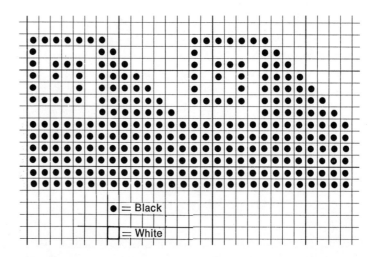

● = Black

□ = White

34

Shape Cap: With White, bind off 5 sts at beg of next 2 rows. Dec 1 st at each edge every other row until 8 (10, 12) sts rem. Bind off. Sew right shoulder seam.

NECKBAND:

With right side facing, size 5 needles, and Brown, k 32 (34, 36) sts on back holder, pick up and k 52 (54, 56) sts along left front edge, place marker, k center st from safety pin, place marker, pick up and k 52 (54, 56) sts along right front edge—136 (142, 148) sts around entire neck edge.

Row 1, wrong side: K 2, p 2 to marker, sl marker, p 1, sl marker, k 2, p 2 to end.

Row 2: Work in ribbed patt as established to within 2 sts of marker, k 2 tog, sl marker, k 1, sl marker, k 2 tog, finish row in ribbing as established. Rep these 2 rows six times more. Bind off.

Finishing: Sew left shoulder, side seams, and sleeve seams. Sew in sleeves.

Woman's Rainbow
Popcorn Pullover

Size:

Directions are for Small. Changes for Medium and Large are in parentheses.

Materials:

Knitting worsted-weight wool: 5 (5, 6) 4-oz. skeins Light Blue.

Leftover scraps (CC) of Purple, Red, Orange, Yellow, Dark Blue, Dark Green, Light Green.

Size H aluminum crochet hook.

Tapestry needles.

Needles:

Sizes 6, 7, and 8, or size to obtain gauge.

Gauge:

3½ sts = 1″, 5½ rows = 1″.

Popcorn Stitch:

Cut leftover scraps of CC into 2½–3-yd. lengths. Hold front piece with right side facing you.

Step 1: Insert crochet hook from wrong side in st. Draw end of CC strand to wrong side, leaving a 3″ end on wrong side to be secured later; leave remaining strand on right side to be used for crochet.

Step 2: Insert hook from right side under strand at top of same st at left of long CC strand. Yo hook, draw lp through, ch 4, insert hook from right side under same strand of same st; yo hook, draw lp through st and lp on hook (sl st made); draw lp on hook to 1″; remove hook.

Step 3: Insert hook from wrong side in same st and in dropped CC lp, draw CC lp through to wrong side (popcorn made). Hold ch at right side, drop lp from hook; from wrong side, draw length of CC strand to wrong side, pick up dropped CC lp and draw strand through lp on hook; pull tightly to fasten. Popcorn st completed.

Step 4: Skip next st (according to chart). Insert hook from right side in next st, draw CC strand through st to right side. Repeat from Step 2 to make popcorn st.

BACK:

With size 6 needles and Light Blue, cast on 56 (60, 64) sts. Work in k 2, p 2 ribbing for 3″, inc 1 st in middle of last row—57 (61, 65) sts. Det Light Blue. Att Purple. Change to size 8 needles. Work 3 rows in st st. Det Purple. Att Light Blue. Work in st st for 15½″ (16″, 16½″) or desired length to underarm.

Armhole Shaping: Bind off 5 sts at beg of next 2 rows. Work in st st until armhole measures 6½″ (7″, 7½″).

Shoulder Shaping: Bind off 5 (5, 6) sts at beg of next 2 rows, 5 (5, 5) sts at beg of next 2 rows, then 4 (5, 5) sts at beg of next 2 rows. Place rem 19 (21, 23) sts on holder.

FRONT:

Work same as back until armholes measure 4½″ (5″, 5½″).

Neck Shaping: On right side k 18 (19, 20) sts, sl center 11 (13, 15) sts on holder. Join a second ball of yarn and k 18 (19, 20) sts. Working both sides at once, dec 1 st at neck edge every other row four times. Work on rem 14 (15, 16) sts, each side, until armholes measure 6½″ (7″, 7½″). Shape shoulders as for back. Starting at center front of sweater, 1″ below armholes, work design in popcorn st following color chart and popcorn st instructions.

SLEEVES:

With size 6 needles and Light Blue, cast on 26 (30, 34) sts. Work in k 2, p 2 ribbing for 3½″. Det Light Blue. Att Purple. Change to size 8 needles, and working in st st inc 4 sts evenly spaced across row—30 (34, 38) sts. Work 2 more rows in Purple Det Purple. Att Light Blue. Work in st st for 8 rows. Inc 1 st at each end every 8 rows nine times—48 (52, 56) sts. Work in st st until sleeves measure about 18½″ (19″, 19½″) or desired length to underarm. Bind off. Sew right shoulder seam.

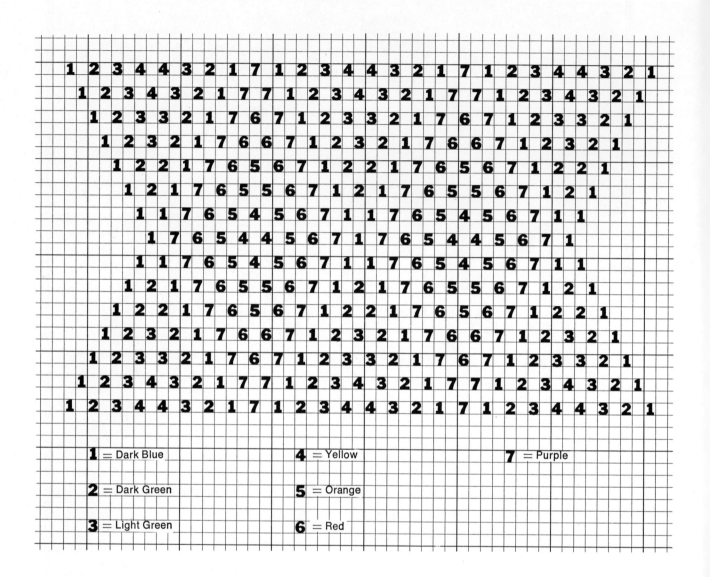

1 2 3 4 4 3 2 1 7 1 2 3 4 4 3 2 1 7 1 2 3 4 4 3 2 1
  1 2 3 4 3 2 1 7 7 1 2 3 4 3 2 1 7 7 1 2 3 4 3 2 1
    1 2 3 3 2 1 7 6 7 1 2 3 3 2 1 7 6 7 1 2 3 3 2 1
      1 2 3 2 1 7 6 6 7 1 2 3 2 1 7 6 6 7 1 2 3 2 1
        1 2 2 1 7 6 5 6 7 1 2 2 1 7 6 5 6 7 1 2 2 1
          1 2 1 7 6 5 5 6 7 1 2 1 7 6 5 5 6 7 1 2 1
            1 1 7 6 5 4 5 6 7 1 1 7 6 5 4 5 6 7 1 1
              1 7 6 5 4 4 5 6 7 1 7 6 5 4 4 5 6 7 1
            1 1 7 6 5 4 5 6 7 1 1 7 6 5 4 5 6 7 1 1
          1 2 1 7 6 5 5 6 7 1 2 1 7 6 5 5 6 7 1 2 1
        1 2 2 1 7 6 5 6 7 1 2 2 1 7 6 5 6 7 1 2 2 1
      1 2 3 2 1 7 6 6 7 1 2 3 2 1 7 6 6 7 1 2 3 2 1
    1 2 3 3 2 1 7 6 7 1 2 3 3 2 1 7 6 7 1 2 3 3 2 1
  1 2 3 4 3 2 1 7 7 1 2 3 4 3 2 1 7 7 1 2 3 4 3 2 1
1 2 3 4 4 3 2 1 7 1 2 3 4 4 3 2 1 7 1 2 3 4 4 3 2 1

1 = Dark Blue   **4** = Yellow   **7** = Purple

2 = Dark Green   **5** = Orange

3 = Light Green   **6** = Red

40

Neckband: With right side facing, with Purple and size 7 needles, pick up and k 17 sts along left front neck edge, 11 (13, 15) sts from center holder, 17 sts along right front neck edge and 19 (21, 23) sts from back holder—64 (68, 72) sts around entire neck edge. With Purple, p 1 row. Det Purple. Att Light Blue. Work in k 2, p 2 ribbing for 6 rows. Bind off loosely in ribbing.

Finishing: Sew left shoulder seam, side seams, and sleeve seams. Sew in sleeves.

Woman's Chenille
V-Neck Pullover

Size:

Directions are for Small size. Changes for Medium and Large sizes are in parentheses.

Materials:

Rayon chenille sport-weight yarn: 8 oz. (8 oz., 9 oz.) Off-White, 8 oz. (9 oz., 10 oz.) Dark Red, 9 oz. (10 oz., 11 oz.) Dark Green.

Tapestry Needle.

Elastic thread.

Entire sweater is worked with 2 strands of chenille yarn.

Needles:

Sizes 6, 7, and 9, or sizes to obtain gauge.

Gauge:

3 sts = 1″, 6 rows = 1″.

Ribbed Pattern Stitch:

Row 1, right side: * P 1, sl 2, rep from * across row, ending p 1.
Row 2: K 1, p 2 across row, ending k 1.

BACK:

With size 7 needles and 2 strands of Off-White, cast on 52 (55, 58) sts. Work in ribbed patt st for 2½″. Change to size 9 needles and att Dark Green. Work in st st: 1 row Dark Green, 2 rows Off-White five times, ending with a Dark Green row. Det Dark Green. Att Dark Red. Work in st st for 7½″ (8″, 8½″). Det Dark Red. Att Off-White. Work in st st for 5 rows. Det Off-White. Att Dark Green, cont until piece measures 16″ (16½″, 17″). Mark with contrasting yarn for armhole. Cont working with Dark Green in st st for 4½″ (5″, 5½″). Det Dark Green. Att Off-White. Work in st st for 7 rows. Det Off-White. Att Dark Green. Cont with Dark Green until armholes measure 6½″ (7″, 7½″).

42

Shoulder Shaping: Bind off 4 (5, 6) sts at beg of next 2 rows, 5 (5, 5) sts at beg of next 2 rows, then 5 (5, 5) sts at beg of next 2 rows. Place rem 24 (25, 26) sts on holder.

FRONT:

Work same as back until entire piece measures 15" (15½", 16").

V-Neck Shaping: Work across 26 (27, 29) sts. In size Medium, k 27th and 28th sts tog. Join a second ball of yarn and k 26 (27, 29) sts. Working both sides at once, dec 1 st at neck edge every 3rd row twelve (twelve, thirteen) times. When armhole measures 4½" (5", 5½"), det Dark Green and att Off-White. Work in st st for 7 rows. Det Off-White. Att Dark Green. Cont with Dark Green until armholes measure 6½" (7", 7½"). Shape shoulders as for back.

SLEEVES:

With size 6 needles and 2 strands of Off-White, cast on 28 (31, 34) sts. Work in ribbed patt st for 3". Change to size 9 needles. Det Off-White. Att Dark Red. Work in st st inc 15 sts evenly spaced across row—43 (46, 49) sts. Work Dark Red in st st for 6" (6½", 7"). Det Dark Red. Work Dark Green and Off-White stripe same as back and front of sweater. Work Dark Green for 6½" (7", 7½"). Bind off. Sleeves should measure 18½" (19½", 20½"). Sew right shoulder seam.

Neckband: Starting at left front edge, with size 6 needles and 2 strands of Off-White, pick up and k 41 (42, 43) sts along neck edge to center of V. Work in ribbed patt st for 8 rows. Bind off. Starting at center with size 6 needles and 2 strands of Off-White, pick up and k 42 (43, 44) sts along right front edge, and k the 24 (25, 26) sts on back holder. Work in ribbed patt st for 8 rows. Bind off.

Finishing: Sew left shoulder seam, side seams, and sleeve seams. Sew in sleeves. Cross neckband at center and sew. Sew elastic thread around neck to hold shape.

Woman's Cape

Size and Measurements:

One size fits all. After steaming, approximate length at front edges and center back, 42"; shoulder to lower edge of center, 33".

Materials:

Hand-spun and hand-dyed yarns: 1 lb. each of Dark Green and White; ½ lb. each of Rust, Blue, Green, Purple, Blue, Yellow, Orange, and Red.

Tapestry needle.

Entire cape is worked with 2 strands of yarn.

Needle:

Size 10 circular.

Gauge:

3 sts = 1", 4 rows = 1".

RIGHT HALF:

Cast on 32 sts with Dark Green.

Row 1: K across to within last 5 sts, p 1, k 1, ending p 1.

Row 2, right side: K 1, p 1, k 1, p 1, k 1, inc 1 st, k across to last st, inc in last st. On right side, inc 1 st after ribbed border and inc 1 st at end of line every other row throughout.

Row 3: K across to last 5 sts, work in rib. Att White (twisting yarn to prevent hole), inc 1 st, k across to last st, inc 1 st in last st (36 sts).

Row 4: Work White in st st for 4 rows. Keep Dark Green border throughout.

Row 8: Det White. Att Rust. K across (40 sts).

Row 9: K across with Rust (42 sts).

Row 10: Det Rust. Att Dark Blue, p 1, * sl 1, p 5 across.

Row 11: Sl 1, inc 1, k 4, * sl 1, k 5 rep from * across (44 sts).

Row 12: P 2, * sl 1, p 5 rep from * across, ending sl 1.

Row 13: Det Dark Blue. Att Light Green. K across (46 sts).

Row 14: Det Light Green. Att Purple. P across.

Row 15: P across (48 sts).

Row 16: P across.

Row 17: Att Light Blue, sl 1, inc 1, k 3, * sl 1, k 4 rep from * across row (50 sts).

Row 18: With Light Blue, * p 4, sl 1 rep from * across (52 sts).

Row 19: Det Light Blue. Pick up Purple, k across.

Row 20: K across in Purple.

Row 21: Det Purple. Att Light Green, k across (52 sts).

Row 22: Det Light Green. Attach Dark Blue, k across.

Row 23: K Dark Blue across (56 sts).

Row 24: P Dark Blue across.

Row 25: Det Dark blue. Att Rust, * k 5, sl 1, rep from * across (58 sts).

Row 26: P Rust sts, sl Dark Blue sts.

Row 27: Det Dark Blue. K Rust across (60 sts).

Row 28: Attach White, p 3, sl 1 * p 5, sl 1, rep from * across.

Row 29: With Rust inc 1, k 3 sl 1, * k 5, sl 1, rep from * ending k 3, inc 1 (62 sts).

Row 30: P Rust sts, sl White sts across.

Row 31: Det Rust, K White across (64 sts).

Row 32: P White across.

Row 33: K White across (66 sts).

Row 34: Att Yellow, p 3 White, p 2 Yellow across.

Row 35: K Yellow sts, k White sts (68 sts).

Row 36: Det Yellow, p White across.

Row 37: Att Dark Green, inc 1 st, k 1 Dark Green, k 4 White across ending k 3 (70 sts).

Row 38: P White sts, p Yellow sts.

Row 39: Det White, k Dark Green across (72 sts).

Row 40: P Dark Green.

Row 41: Det Dark Green, Att Light Blue, k across (74 sts).

Row 42: K Light Blue across.

Row 43: Attach Red, sl 1 Light Blue, inc 1 Red, k 3 Red, * sl 1 Light Blue, k 4, rep from * across (76 sts).

Row 44: Sl Light Blue sts, p Red sts.

Row 45: Det Red, k Light Blue across (78 sts).

Row 46: K Light Blue across.

Row 47: Det Light Blue, k Dk Green across (80 sts).

Row 48: P Dark Green across.

Row 49: Att Rust, k 1 Dark Green, k 5 Rust across (82 sts).

Row 50: P Rust sts, sl Dark Green sts across.

Row 51: K Rust across (84 sts).

Row 52: Det Rust. Att White, * sl 1, p 5 White across.

Row 53: Work White above White sts, sl Rust sts across (86 sts).

Rows 54 through 61: Work White in st st.

Row 62: K White across.

Row 63: K White across (96 sts).

Row 64: Det White. Att Dark Blue and k across.

Rows 65 through 76: Work in garter st as follows:

2 rows Dark Blue, 2 rows Light Green, 2 rows Purple, 2 rows Light Blue, 2 rows Dark Green, 2 rows Orange.

Row 77: Det Orange. Att White, * k 5 White, sl 1 Orange * across row (110 sts).

Row 78: P White sts, sl Orange sts.

Rows 79 to 81: Work White in st st. Rep Rows 8 to 60 (166 sts). Work in garter st as follows:

2 rows White, 2 rows Orange, 4 rows Rust, 4 rows Dark Blue, 2 rows Light Green, 4 rows Purple, 2 rows Light Blue, 4 rows Dark Green (190 sts). Bind off.

Finishing: Weave center back seam. With Purple make popcorn sts on 2 White stripes. Make 1 popcorn st every 5th st, centering Rust sl sts. Weave all ends in.

Braided Ties: With 12 strands of yarn, make braid 18″ long. Sew braids to top corners of Dark Green border.

Pat yourself on the back . . .

Dione Christensen

If you've seen the book Knitting, then you've seen Dione Christensen's knitting, even if you didn't look inside: The entire cover is a close-up of one of her immediately recognizable sweaters. And if you've seen the cover of Elyse Sommer's A New Look at Knitting, you've seen Dione herself: She's pictured on the cover wearing another of her designs. Before becoming the knitting world's cover person, Dione studied textile design in California where she also became interested in knitting and crochet. In New York she began developing the intricate color schemes in basic sweater designs that have become her personal trademark. She shows regularly at New York's prestigious Julie: Artisans' Gallery and her work was included in the inaugural exhibition at the brand new SoHo (New York) craft gallery, Makers Gallery. Magazines featuring Dione's designs have included Family Circle and Gentlemen's Quarterly.

50

"There are a lot of innovative things being done in knitting these days: very contemporary designs are becoming almost as accepted, I think, as the old traditional ones—the ones we always refer to as the classics. There's no single source for most of my design ideas. I get a lot of ideas from looking at art: paintings —the patterned sweater was inspired by a painting in the Metropolitan Museum of Art, Hartley's Prussian Officer—prints, and sculpture with textured surfaces that sometimes look almost like knitting. And forms in nature sometimes turn into knitting ideas. I do many drawings of things around me that might be translatable into knitting and I return to these sketches when I'm planning something new.

"I never think about how difficult a design might be to execute. I'm always experimenting to find out what will work in a knitted piece, and equally important, what won't work. I prefer to put a complicated image on a simple sweater and a complicated structure on a wall piece. Some very creative fiber artists are making garments today that are hardly garments at all; they're more like works of art than wearable pieces and they're more at home behind glass or in a Plexiglas box than on a body. As works of art they're very exciting. But there's a thin line dividing that kind of craftwork and truly wearable garments, and a lot of people today seem to be treading that line. I think it's important to do both."

Dione Christensen

Marsden Hartley Sweater

Size:

Directions are for Medium sizes (40 to 42). Changes for Large (44 to 46) and Extra-Large (48 to 50) are in parentheses.

Chest Measurements:

After blocking, 44″ (48″, 52″).

Materials:

Knitting worsted, 4-oz. skeins.

Mint (D)	1 skein
Black (B)	1 skein
Dark Red (G)	1 skein
Ivory (C)	1 skein
French Blue (E)	1 skein
Gold (F)	1 skein
Plum (A)	2 skeins

Sport-weight wool, 2-oz. skeins.

Dark Moss (D)	1 skein
Medium Blue (E)	1 skein
Charcoal Gray (B)	1 skein
Ivory (C)	1 skein
Red (G)	1 skein
Gold (F)	1 skein
Dark Blue Gray (A)	2 skeins

2 Stitch holders.

Needles:

Sizes 8 and 11; size 8 dp.

Gauge:

7 sts = 2″; 9 rows = 2″.

Materials Note: Two strands of yarn (1 worsted and 1 sport-weight) are always worked together. The following combinations are worked as indicated. Before beginning, wind together 5 balls Ivory worsted and Ivory sport-weight, 5 Dark Red and Red, 4 Plum and Dark Blue Gray, 4 Black and Charcoal Gray, 4 Dark Moss and Mint, 4 French Blue and Medium Blue, 3 Gold and Gold.

BACK:

Follow chart (page 55) for back throughout. With size 8 needles and Plum and Blue Gray, cast on, 62 (66, 70) sts. Work in k 1, p 1 rib for 10 rows. Inc 1 st at end of last row—63 (67, 71) sts. Change to size 11 needles and k pattern in st st for 66 (68, 70) rows.

Shape Armholes: Bind off 4 sts beg of next 2 rows. Dec 1 st each side every other row twice. Work even for 36 (38, 40) rows.

Shape Shoulders: Bind off 8 (9, 10) sts next 2 rows, 9 (9, 10) sts next 2 rows. Sl rem 17 (19, 21) sts onto holder.

FRONT:

(Following chart (page 56) k same as back until 18 (20, 22) rows above 1st bound-off armhole sts.

Shape Neck: K 22 (23, 25) sts, Sl center 7 (9, 9) sts onto holder. Join another ball of yarn, and keeping to patt, finish row. Working on both sides at once, dec 1 st at neck edge every other row five times. Work even until armhole measures same as back.

Shape Shoulders: Bind off 8 (9, 10) sts beg of each arm side once, 9 (9, 10) sts once.

SLEEVES:

With size 8 needles and Plum and Blue Gray, cast on 34 sts. Work in k 1, p 1 rib for 10 rows, inc 1 st at end of last row. Change to size 11 needles and following chart (pages 57 and 58), work in st st, inc 1 st each side every 8th row 7 (8, 9) times. Work for 76 (80, 82) rows.

Shape Cap: Bind off 3 (4, 4) sts beg of next 2 rows. Dec 1 st each side every other row until 23 (21, 21) sts. Bind off 3 sts at beg of next 4 rows. Bind off rem 11 (9, 9) sts.

Finishing: Steam-press pieces lightly. With 2 strands of yarn backstitch both shoulder seams.

Neckband: With dp needles, pick up 20 (22, 22) sts on left front neck edge, pick up sts on front holder, 20 (22, 22) sts on right front edge, pick up sts on back holder 64 (72, 74) sts. Work in k 1, p 1 ribbing for 5 rows. Bind off loosely in ribbing, using size 11 needles. Fasten. Sew side seams and sleeve seams. Sew in sleeves.

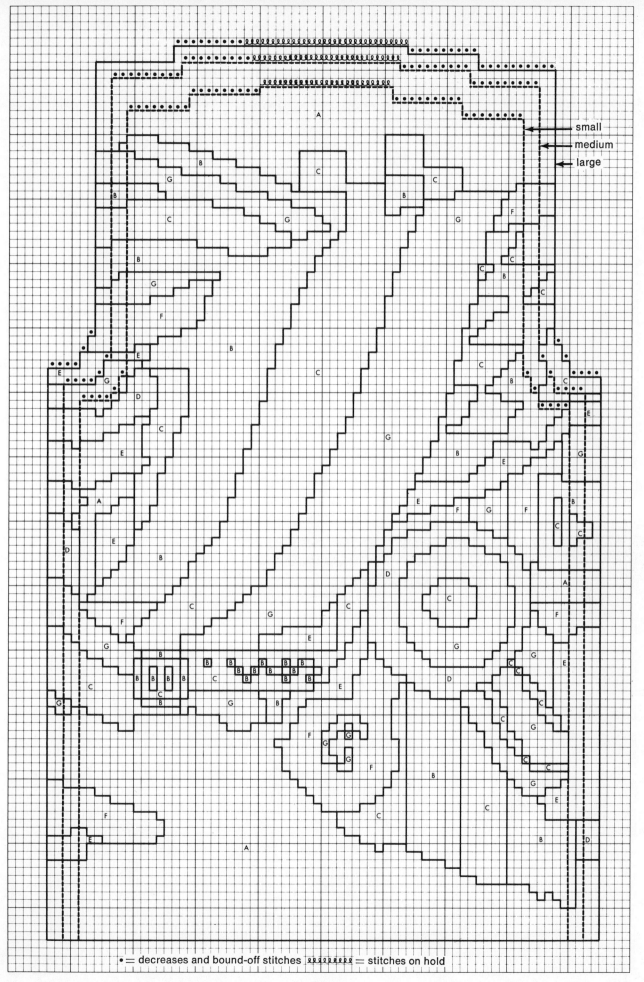

small

medium

large

A

B

G

B

C

B

C

G

C

B

C

B

G

F

C

B

C

C

B

E

E

E

G

D

C

E

D

C

A

E

E

B

C

G

F

F

B

G

G

F

G

E

G

C

C

B

B B B B B B B B B B B B B B

C

C

B

G

B

F

G G

G

F

D

A

B

E

D

G

C

E

C

E

B

C

G

C

C

C

C

G

C

C

G

E

B

D

F

E

A

C

A

B

D

• = decreases and bound-off stitches ⦚⦚⦚⦚⦚⦚⦚⦚ = stitches on hold

BACK

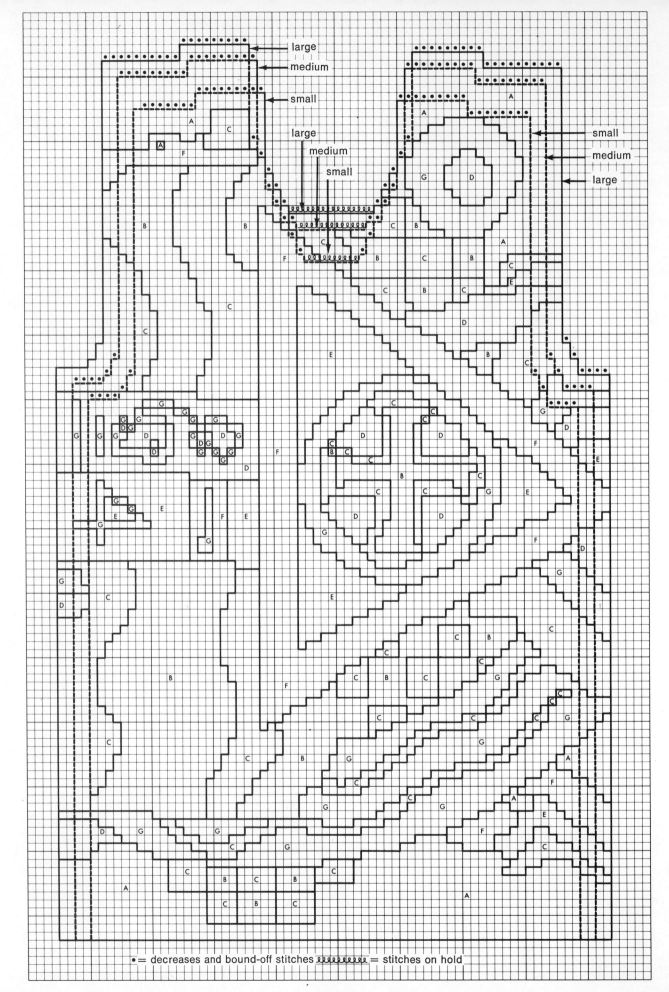

large

medium

small

large
medium
small

small
medium
large

A

A

A

C

A

F

D

G

B

B

G

C

B

C

C

B

A

C

C

B

C

F

B

E

C

B

C

E

D

D

G

G

G

C

B

E

G

G

G

D

D

G

G

D

G

D

C

C

C

C

B

C

E

G

C

G

G

D

D

G

E

D

D

D

C

G

E

F

G

C

F

E

F

E

G

G

E

D

E

C

G

G

B

C

B

C

C

C

C

B

C

C

C

B

C

C

G

C

D

B

F

G

C

G

C

G

C

B

C

B

G

A

C

G

C

F

D

A

G

A

E

D

G

G

C

F

B

A

F

D

C

B

C

C

B

C

A

A

C

B

C

• = decreases and bound-off stitches ꙮꙮꙮꙮꙮ = stitches on hold

FRONT

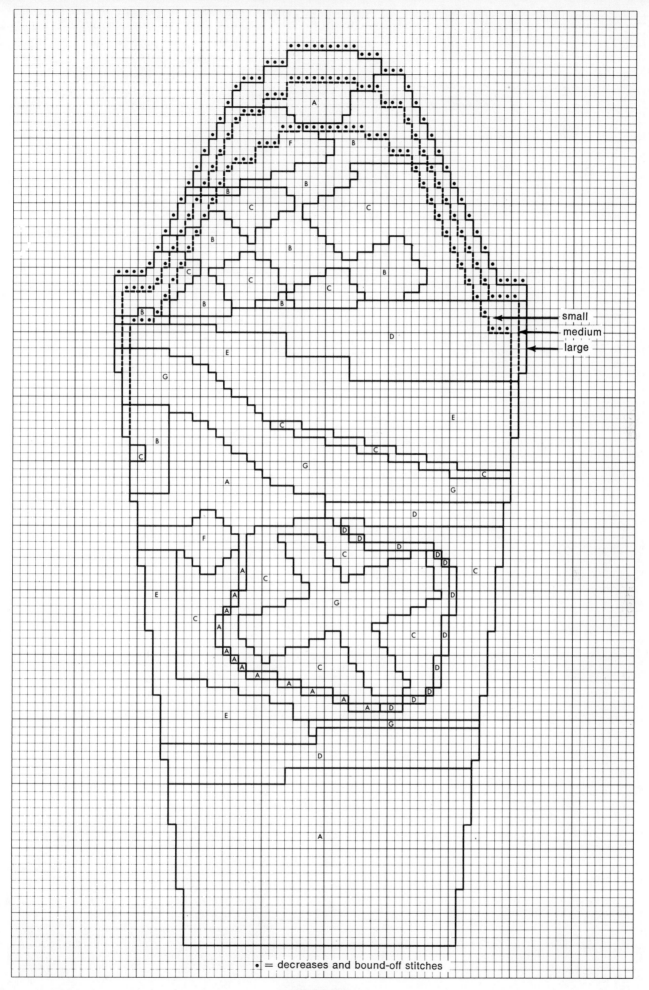

small
medium
large

• = decreases and bound-off stitches

RIGHT SLEEVE

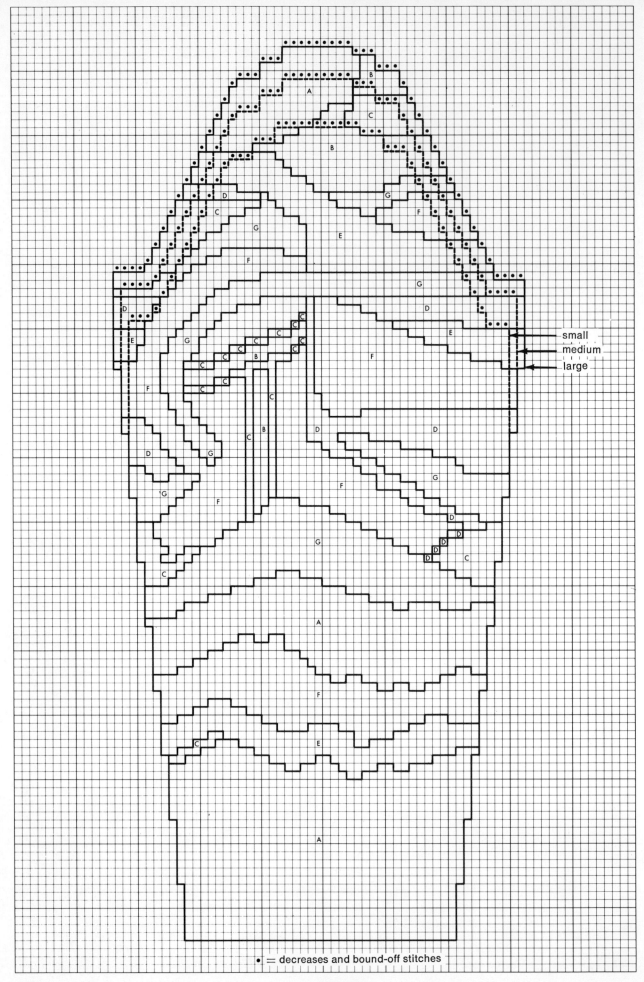

small
medium
large

● = decreases and bound-off stitches

LEFT SLEEVE

Ribbon Vest

Size:

Directions are for Small sizes (6 to 8). Changes for Medium (10 to 12) and Large (14 to 16) are in parentheses.

Chest measurements:

After blocking, 32″ (34″, 36″).

Materials:

Knitting worsted, 4-oz. skeins.

Gray Heather (GH)	1 skein
Maroon (M)	1 skein
Pale Pink (PP)	1 skein
Salmon (S)	1 skein

Sport-weight wool, 2-oz. skeins.

Red (R)	1 skein
Ivory (I)	1 skein

1 gross #2 Rattail Bright Green (RAT).
100 yds. Rose Acetate Ribbon (ACE).
1 gross Baby Slide Cord Black (SLIDE).
1 tube Silver Metallic (MET) Cordinette.
2 Stitch holders.

Needles:

Sizes 8 and 11; size 8 circular.

Gauge:

Stockinette stitch, 7 sts = 2″; 9 rows = 2″.

BACK:

With size 8 needles cast on 44 (54, 62) sts, with single strand GH. work in garter st for 26 (30, 30) rows, inc 1 st end of last row—45 (55, 63) sts. Change to size 11 needles and work in st st and garter st for 38 (40, 40) rows following pattern: St st 3 rows GH and S, on wrong side k 1 row RAT and SLIDE. St st 4 rows GH and S, 3 rows R and S, on wrong side, k 1 row RAT and

MET. St st 4 rows R and S, 3 rows R and PP. On wrong side k 1 row SLIDE and MET. St st 4 rows R and PP, 3 rows M and PP. On wrong side k 1 row ACE and SLIDE. St st 4 rows M and PP, 3 rows M and R. On wrong side, k 1 row ACE and MET. St st 4 rows M and R, 3 rows R and PP. On wrong side, k RAT and ACE. St st 4 rows R and PP, 3 rows PP and W. On wrong side, k 1 row RAT and SLIDE. St st 4 rows W and PP, 3 rows M and W. On wrong side, k 1 row Ace and Met. St st 4 rows M and W, 3 rows M and S. On wrong side, k 1 row RAT and MET. St st 4 rows M and S, 3 rows S and PP. On wrong side, k 1 row SLIDE and ACE—76 rows. Finish large size with 4 rows S and PP.

Armhole Shaping: Bind off 4 sts at beg of next 2 rows. Dec 4 sts each side every other row two (four, four) times. Work even until 32 (34, 36) rows from first bound-off sts. Right side facing, bind off 4 (4, 5) sts beg of next 2 rows, 4 (5, 6) sts next 2 rows. Sl rem 15 (21, 25) sts on holder.

FRONT:

Work same as back until 8 (10, 12) rows above first bound-off armhole sts.

Neckline Shaping: K 13 (14, 16) sts, sl 7 (11, 15) sts on holder, att another double strand of yarn, finish row. Working on both sides at once with separate strands of yarn, dec 1 st at neck edge every other row five times, 8 (9, 11) sts each side. Work even until armholes are same as back.

Shape Shoulders: Bind off 4 (4, 5) sts at beg of each arm side once, then 4 (5, 6) sts once.

Finishing: Steam-press pieces lightly on back. With double strand of yarn sew up shoulder and side seams using back st.

NECKBAND:

Using circular needle, join yarn (single strand GH) on left front edge and pick up 23 (25, 25) sts on left front neck edge, k sts on front holder, pick up 23 (25, 25) sts on right front, k sts on back holder 68 (82, 90) sts. Working in rounds, alternate k and p rows for 5 rows. Using size 8 straight needles, bind off sts loosely.

SLEEVEBAND:

Using circular needle and single strand GH, pick up 64 (68, 72) sts around armhole edge. Alternate k and p rnds for 5 rnds. Bind off loosely using size 8 straight needles. Fasten off.

Chinese Jacket

Size:

Directions are for Small sizes (8 to 10). Changes for Medium (12 to 14) and Large (16 to 18) are in parentheses.

Chest measurements:

After blocking 34″ (36″, 38″).

Materials:

Knitting worsted, 4-oz. skeins.

Black (B)	3 skeins
Gray Heather (GH)	1 skein
Golf Green (GG)	1 skein
Dark Green (DG)	1 skein
Navy (N)	1 skein
Rose (R)	1 skein
Scarlet (S)	1 skein
Cardinal (C)	1 skein
Dark Blue (DG)	1 skein

1 gross #2 Rattail Bright Green (RAT).
100 yds. Rose Acetate Ribbon (ACE).
1 gross Baby Slide Cord Black (SLIDE).
1 tube Silver Metallic Cordinette (MET).
1 stitch holder.

Needles:

Size 11, or size to obtain gauge.

Gauge:

Stockinette st, 7 sts = 2″; 9 rows = 2″.

Pattern:

Starts at lower edge of sleeve after border. St st 7 rows GG and C. One row RAT and SLIDE knitted on wrong side (garter row), 7 rows GG and DB. One row RAT and MET, 7 rows S and DB. One row RAT and ACE. Jacket body starts and sleeve continues. Seven rows S and C. One row Rat and MET, 7 rows C and DG.

One row RAT and ACE, 7 rows DG and GG. One row RAT and SLIDE, 7 rows GG and GH. One row RAT and ACE, 7 rows GH and R. One row RAT and SLIDE, 7 rows R and DB. One row RAT and MET, 7 rows DB and N. One row RAT and ACE, 7 rows N and DG. One row RAT and MET, 7 rows DG and S. One row RAT and SLIDE, 7 rows S and R. One row RAT and MET. Last rows R and GG.

BACK:

With size 11 needles and triple strand of Black, cast on 50 (54, 62) sts. Work in garter st for 12 rows. Follow patt for 46 (48, 48) rows.

Shape Armholes: Bind off 2 (3, 4) sts at beg of next 2 rows. Dec 1 st each side every other row twice. Work even for 34 (36, 38) rows.

Shape Shoulders: Bind off 5 (6, 8) sts beg of next 2 rows, 8 sts next 2 rows. Sl rem 16 (18, 18) sts on holder.

RIGHT FRONT:

With size 11 needles and triple strand of Black, cast on 32 (34, 38) sts. Work in garter st for 12 rows. Continue with garter st at front edge for border 7 sts, and at same time work patt until piece measures same as back.

Shape Armholes: Bind off 2 (3, 4) sts at arm edge once. Dec 1 st at arm edge every other row twice. Work even until 30 (32, 34) rows completed.

Shape Neck: At front edge bind off 13 (13, 14) sts, finish row. Dec 1 st at neck edge every other row twice. Work even until armhole is 34 (36, 38) rows.

Shape Shoulders: At arm edge bind off 5 (6, 8) sts once, 8 sts once.

LEFT FRONT:

Work same as for right, reversing shaping.

SLEEVES:

With triple strand of Black, cast on 44 (46, 48) sts. Work in garter st for 12 rows. Following patt work even until 70 (72, 72) rows completed.

Shape Cap: Bind off 2 (3, 4) sts beg of next 2 rows. Dec 1 st each side every other row until 20 (20, 22) sts. Bind off 3 sts at beg of next 4 rows. Bind off rem 8 (8, 10) sts.

Finishing: Steam-press pieces lightly on wrong side. With 2 strands of yarn, sew up both shoulder seams. Sew sleeve seams.

NECKBAND:

Att 3 strands Black at right front neck edge. Pick up 19 (19, 20) sts on right front neck edge, sts on back holder, 19 (19, 20) sts on left front neck edge. K 11 rows garter st, dec 1 st at shoulder every other row—44 (46, 48) sts. Bind off sts. Fasten. Sew side body seams. Sew in sleeves.

TIES:

Cut 192″ lengths, 1 each of GG, N, R, S, and MET. Follow general rope directions. Cut eight 12″ lengths from rope. Knot each end of each piece. On right front border, sew on one piece at edge of neckband in center. One opposite 3rd garter row from top at border edge. One opposite 6th garter row from top. One opposite 9th garter row from top. On left front border, sew on piece 3″ in from neckband edge (center). One on 3rd garter row from top, 3″ in from front border edge. One on 6th garter row from top, 3″ in from front border edge. One on 9th garter row from top, 3″ in from front border edge.

GENERAL DIRECTIONS FOR ROPE

Tie one end of yarn to a doorknob. Stretch yarn out and trim ends evenly. With bobby pin, pull ends through hole of a thread spool (large spool will be needed for heavy yarn). Make a knot. Slip a pencil through strands of yarn between spool and knot. Holding the spool, twist yarn tightly by twirling pencil. As you twist yarn move in as yarn contracts (don't let yarn kink). When yarn is twisted tightly, find center of rope and keeping yarn taut, bring yarn around a chair folding in half. Remove pencil and spool and twist yarn in opposite direction to form rope, keeping rope taut and moving fingers down rope as it twists. Cut yarn at both ends and knot.

Indian Spirit Cape

Size:

One size fits all.

Materials:

Knitting worsted, 4-oz. skeins.

Light Gray (LG)	2 skeins
Gray Heather (GH)	2 skeins
Black (B)	2 skeins
Navy (N)	2 skeins
Dark Blue (DB)	1 skein
Royal Blue (RB)	1 skein
Purple (P)	1 skein
Cardinal (C)	1 skein
Scarlet (S)	1 skein
Orange (O)	1 skein
Yellow Orange (YO)	1 skein
Light Yellow Orange (LYO)	1 skein
Green (G)	1 skein

Needles:

Size 11 circular 36″; size 11 straight.

Gauge:

7 sts = 2″; 9 rows = 2″. Back neck length = 48″ with 3″ allowance for stretch. Width around lower edge = 100″.

Pattern:

Forty rows B and N, 10 rows N and DB. Next 3 rows follow chart I. Three rows N and DB. One row each DB and P, P and C, C and S, S and O. Ten rows P and DB. One row each RB and G, G and S, S and O, O and YO. Six rows DB and P. Ten rows P and RB. Four rows garter st, 1 row each RB and GH, O and GH, O and YO, YO and LYO. Six rows st st LG and GH. Next 24 rows follow chart II. To beg wind 10 balls yarn S and C, 9 balls YO and LYO. Cont with LG and GH to end.

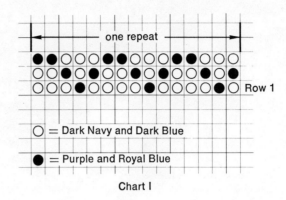

Chart I

◯ = Dark Navy and Dark Blue

● = Purple and Royal Blue

BACK:

With double strand B and N, cast on 128 sts with circular needle. Work in st st for 8 rows.

Row 9: Dec 1 st at beg and end of row. Then dec 1 st at beg and end of every 8th row three times. Rep dec every 6th row eleven times (mark 9th dec row for arm opening. Dec every 4th row six times (86 sts). Mark last dec row for end of arm opening. Dec 1 st at beg and end of every other row eight times (70 sts).

Next 7 rows: Dec 1 st at each end of every row, ending with a p row (56 sts).

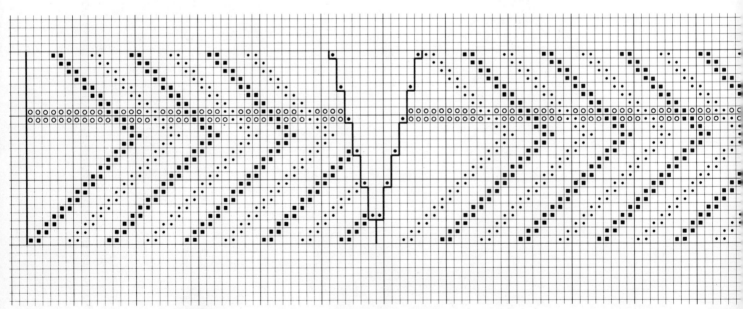

Chart II

Shape Shoulders and Neck: Bind off 3 sts at beg of next 4 rows (44 sts).

Next row: Bind off 2 sts at beg of next 6 rows. Bind off 2 sts at beg of next row, k 6, drop yarn, att new yarn and bind off 16 sts (for neck), k across. Bind off 2 sts at beg of next row. Dec 1 st at each neck edge and 2 sts at shoulder edges every row until 3 sts remain. Bind off.

RIGHT FRONT:

With double strand B and N, cast on 60 sts using size 11 straight needles. Work in st st for 8 rows.

Row 9: Dec 1 st at end of row (place marker for side edge), then every 8th row three times (56 sts), every 6th row eleven times (mark 9th dec. row for arm opening), every 4th row six times (39 sts). Place a marker in last dec row for end of arm opening. Dec 1 st arm side every other row eight times (31 sts), every row seven times (24 sts).

Shape Neck: Bind off 3 sts at side edge every other row twice (18 sts). Bind off 2 sts at front edge and 2 sts at side edge until 5 sts remain.

Next row: Bind off 2 sts at side edge. Bind off remaining sts.

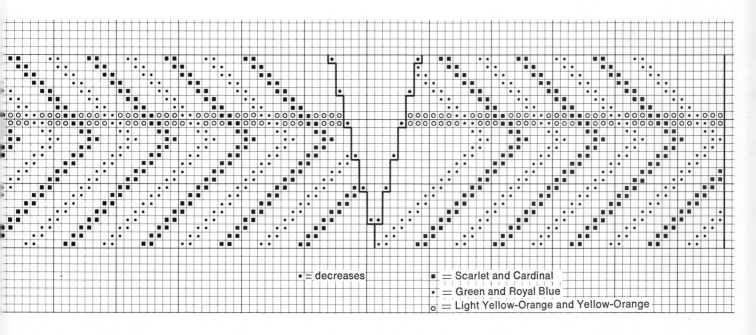

• = decreases

■ = Scarlet and Cardinal
• = Green and Royal Blue
○ = Light Yellow-Orange and Yellow-Orange

LEFT FRONT:

Work same as right reversing shaping.

Finishing: Steam-press pieces lightly. Sew in all loose ends of yarn on wrong side. With 2 strands sew side seams, leaving armholes open where marked. Turn in approx ¼″ for hem on armhole edge. Sew on wrong side.

LOWER BORDER:

With circular needle and 3 strands O, YO, LYO, cast on 246 sts and k 1 row. Next 9 rows: 1 Row each YO, O, G/G, O, RB/RB, G, C/RB, C, S/RB, O, S/RB, G, S/G, S, GH/GH, LG, S/GH, LG, C. Bind off sts. Sew border to lower edge of cape.

FRONT BORDERS:

With 3 strands GH, LG, LYO, cast on 5 sts on size 11 straight needles. Work in garter st for 20 rows. Change GH to YO, k in garter st for 30 rows, change LG to O, work 20 rows, change LYO to S, work 10 rows, change YO to C, work 10 rows, change O to P, work 20 rows, change S to RB, work 10 rows, change C to G, work 10 rows, change P to N, work 10 rows, change RB to B work 17 rows. Bind off sts. Steam-press pieces stretching them to match cape length. Sew borders to right and left front edges, gray area at bottom.

NECKBAND:

Attach DB, N, RB at right neck edge. Pick up 5 sts on border, 12 sts neck edge, 21 sts neck back, 12 sts left neck edge, 5 sts border. Working in garter st, k 10 rows, dec 1 st at shoulders every other row four times. Bind off sts.

TIE:

Cut 120″, 5 strands—O, G, C, S, LYO. Follow directions for rope on page 65. Sew tie evenly along bottom edge of neckband.

Carpet Bag

Size:

Body of bag folded in half, 12″ h × 13″ w.

Materials:

6-ply rug yarn, 4-oz. skeins.

Ivory (A)	1 skein
Apple Green (A)	1 skein
Cardinal (A)	1 skein
Heather Gray (B)	2 skeins
Scarlet and Rose (C)	1 skein
Royal Blue and Forest Green (D)	1 skein

Size K aluminum crochet hook.
12″-long wooden stick handles.

Needles:

Size 15.

Gauge:

2½ sts = 1″, 4½ rows = 1″.

Pattern:

A, garter st; B, st st; C, garter st; D, st st.

BAG BODY:

With size 15 needles, cast on 30 sts—10 sts A, 10 sts B, 10 sts A. Work in patt for 10 rows, change to D–10 sts, C–10 sts, D–10 sts. Work for 10 rows, change to C–10 sts, D–10 sts, C–10 sts, work for 10 rows. Change to B–10 sts, A–10 sts, B–10 sts, work for 10 rows. Change to A–10 sts, B–10 sts, A–10 sts, B–10 sts, work for 10 rows. Change to A–10 sts, B–10 sts, A–10 sts, work for 10 rows. Change to D–10 sts, C–10 sts, D–10 sts, work for 10 rows. Change to A–10 sts, D–10 sts, A–10 sts, work for 10 rows. Change to B–10 sts, C–10 sts, B–10 sts, work for 10 rows. Change to C–10 sts, B–10 sts, C–10 sts, work for 10 rows. Bind off sts.

Finishing: With crochet hook and ABA end of bag, attach C to right corner. Long sc over 1 wood handle, working along ABA end. At CBC end attach D, and long sc over second handle working along CBC end. Attach Ivory yarn at right-hand corner at top. With crochet hook sc in top of long sc sts fourteen times, ch 3 (center), finish 14 sc on row, ch 5, turn. In 3rd ch from hook * sc, ch 5, sk 2; rep from * three times, 7 dc in center ch, * sk 2, sc, ch 5; rep from * three times, ch 3, sc in end st, ch 1 turn. * Sc in top of ch, ch 2; rep from * three times, 2 dc in each center dc (14) dc, sc in top of ch; rep from * three times, end off. Rep patt on other side of bag. Fold bag in half evenly. Using a single strand of yarn and overcast st, sew up sides to within a square and a half from top edges. Cut thirty-four 6″ pieces of A, sixteen 6″ pieces of C. With crochet hook and 2 strands at a time, hook fringe using A into folded center of each A square at bottom edge of bag, 10 fringes each square. Hook 3 A and 3 C fringes on each side of bag, 10 fringes each square. Hook 3 A and 3 C fringes on each side of bag where A and C squares meet. At top sides of bag, hook 5 A fringes, sides of each A square and 5 C fringes of each C square.

Straps: Cut twelve 90″ lengths 2 A, 2 C, 2 D. Follow directions for rope on page 65. Make 2 straps using 6 strands each (one in each color for each strap). Sl loop at one end of rope around end of wood handle and tie loose ends around other end of wood handle. Repeat on other side.

Phoebe Fox

JEFFREY FOX

Phoebe Fox has worked on the design staffs of both McCall's Needlework and Crafts and American Home magazines. She now works on the other side of the fence as a free-lance designer for such magazines as Seventeen, American Home Crafts, Ladies' Home Journal Needle & Craft, and Woman's Day. Phoebe's work was featured in the book Knitting and in the very popular Family Creative Workshop series. Her work has also been exhibited at the Museum of Contemporary Crafts. Her husband, Jeffrey, the man behind the camera for this book, is a commercial magazine photographer who shares Phoebe's enthusiasm for crafts and has been responsible for many American Home Crafts picture spreads.

"I believe every knitter must have at least one good knitting story to tell. When I was a child, my mother began a sweater using very good yarn. Years later the sweater was still unfinished, but the yarn was perfectly good and the color had mellowed beautifully. So I pulled the yarn out, unkinked it by wetting it and winding it on a piece of cardboard, and used it to knit a brand new sweater for myself. The new sweater was, of course, much larger than the baby sweater—I had grown some—but because I used a very lacy stitch, I had just enough yarn. Only four inches were left over.

"My knitting has come a long way since I made my third sweater out of my first and I feel I've developed a style of my own. I like to think of my work as incorporating design elements that aren't usually thought of as going together. Unusual combinations of stitches and textures and pattern areas are what I strive for. It's this kind of variation that not only keeps a garment interesting, but makes the actual knitting less boring and more enjoyable to do. I enjoy my knitting and I want the people who work my designs to enjoy knitting them, too."

Phoebe Fox

Child's Cardigan and Hat with Duplicate Stitch Motifs

Sizes:

Directions are for sizes 2 to 3. Changes for sizes 4 to 5 and 6 to 7 are in parentheses.
Chest Size: 21″ to 22″ (22½″ to 23½″; 24″ to 25″).
Finished Measurements: 23″ (24½″ 26″).

Materials:

Knitting worsted-weight yarn.

Golden Yellow (A)	4 (5, 6) oz.
White (B)	3 (4, 5) oz.
Purple (C)	4 (5, 6) oz.
Turquoise (D)	½ oz.
Red-Orange (E)	½ oz.
Black (F)	½ oz.

Sizes F and G aluminum crochet hooks.
7 Small buttons.
Tapestry needle.

Needles:

Sizes 5 and 7, or sizes to obtain gauge.

Gauge:

Stockinette st on size 7 needles: 19 sts = 4″.

Sweater

BACK:

With size 5 needles and A, cast on 56 (60, 64) sts. Work in k 1, p 1 ribbing for 1 row. Attach B, leaving A at side. Work 2 rows of ribbing with B, 2 rows A, 2 rows B, 2 rows A; inc 1 st at end of

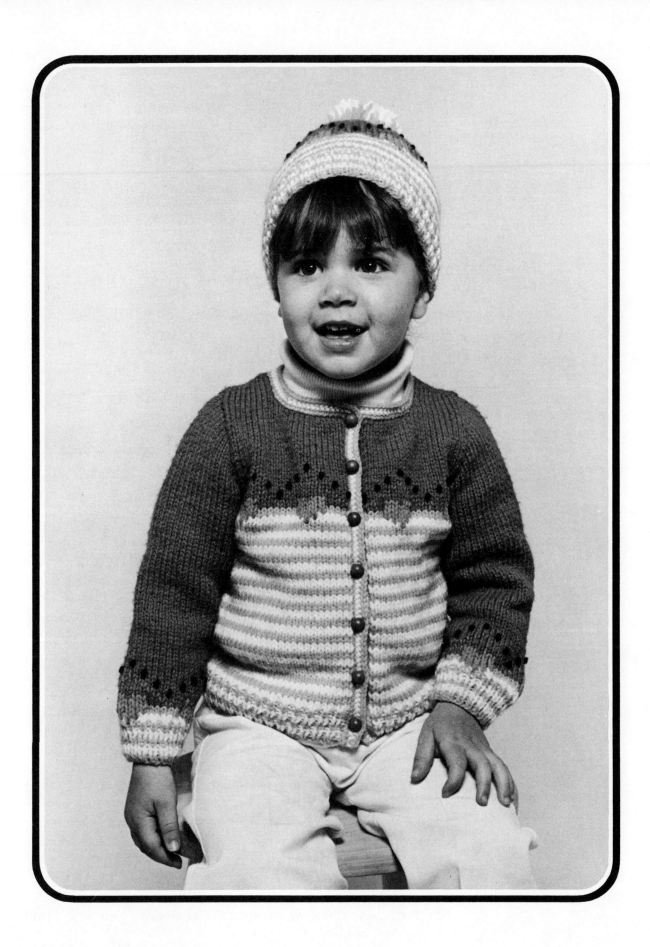

last row—57 (61, 65) sts. Change to size 7 needles and st st, working 2 rows B, 2 rows A for stripes until 8½″ (9½″, 10½″) from beg, or desired length to underarm, ending with p row of A. Fasten off A and B, attach C.

Shape Armholes: Bind off 3 sts at beg of next 2 rows. Dec 1 st at each end every other row three times—45 (49, 53) sts. Work even until armhole measures 3¾″ (4″, 4¼″), ending with a p row. K next row, binding off center 19 (21, 23) sts.

Shape Neck: Working on one side only—13 (14, 15) sts—dec 1 st at neck edge every other row two times. Work even until length is 4¾″ (5″, 5¼″) above first row of armhole shaping.

Shape Shoulders: At arm edge, bind off 6 sts once, then 5 (6, 7) sts once. Attach C to other side of neck and work to correspond.

RIGHT FRONT:

With size 5 needles and A, cast on 30 (32, 34) sts. (Rib as for back, but do not inc 1 st after ribbing.) Work as for back until armhole measures 3¼″ (3½″, 3¾″).

Shape Neck: At neck edge, bind off 11 (12, 13) sts. Dec 1 st at neck edge every other row two times. Work even until front is same length as back. Shape shoulder as for back.

LEFT FRONT:

Work to correspond to right front, reversing shaping.

SLEEVES:

With size 5 needles and A, cast on 38 sts. Rib as for back; inc 1 st at end of ribbing. Change to size 7 needles and st st, work 2 rows B, 2 rows A. Fasten off A and B, attach C. Work even until 2½″ from beg of sleeve. Inc 1 st each end of next row, then every 2″ (1¼″, 1″) until 45 (49, 51) sts. Work even until 9½″ (11″, 12″) from beg, or desired length to underarm.

Shape Cap: Bind off 3 sts at beg of next 2 rows. Dec 1 st at each end every other row eight (nine, ten) times. Bind off 2 sts at beg of next 4 rows. Bind off 3 sts at beg of next 2 rows. Bind off rem 9 (11, 11) sts.

Finishing: Sew shoulder seams. Sew in sleeves. Sew side and undersleeve seams.

Edging:

Row 1: Attach A to lower right front and with G hook, loosely sl st along right front, neck and left front. Make sure that work lies flat. Ch 1, turn.

Row 2: With F hook and A, work 1 sc in each sl st and 3 sc in corner sts to turn. End off. Note: Buttonholes are made on right front for girls and left front for boys. Mark for 7 evenly spaced buttonholes along front edge.

Row 3: With F hook and B, work 1 sc in each sc, 3 sc in corner sts to turn and 7 buttonholes.

Buttonholes: Ch 2, skp 1 st, sc in next st. Fasten off B.

Row 4: With A, work 1 sc in each sc, 3 sc in corner sts, sc in neck sts, taking in slightly to fit, and 2 sc in each ch 2 space for buttonholes. Fasten off. Sew buttons to front edge opposite buttonholes. Weave in all ends.

Embroidery: With tapestry needle and E, follow chart for duplicate st motifs. Starting at point X on chart, work first E st on top of C st that is next to crochet edge. Follow chart, completing 2 motifs on each front. Work 1 French knot with F, 2 sts above every other E st, as shown on chart. Work 4 motifs on back of sweater, to correspond, placing point X on middle st. Work 3 motifs on each sleeve, placing point Y on middle st.

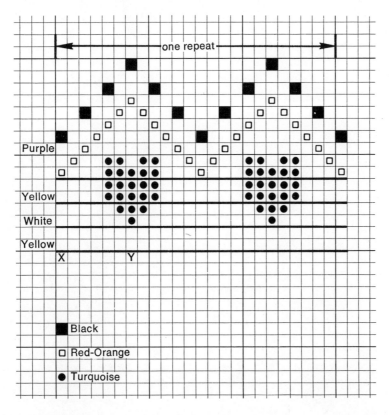

Hat

With size 7 needles and A, loosely cast on 80 (87, 87) sts. Change to size 5 needles and rib as for back. Change to size 7 needles and st st. Work 1 B stripe, 1 A stripe; then dec 1 st at 1 edge every other row five (seven, two) times—75 (80–85) sts. Continue st st stripes until approx 3½″ (4″, 4½″) from beg. Fasten off A and B, attach C.

Dec Row 1: * K 3, k 2 tog. Rep from * across. P 1 row, k 1 row, p 1 row.

Dec Row 2: * K 2, k 2 tog. Rep from * across. P 1 row, k 1 row, p 1 row.

Dec Row 3: * K 1, k 2 tog. Rep from * across. P 1 row.

Dec Row 4: * K 2 tog. Rep from * across. P 1 row.

Dec Row 5: K 0 (k 1, k 2), * k 3 tog. Rep from * across—5 (6, 7) sts are left. End off, leaving an 18″ end. With a tapestry needle, draw yarn through sts andpull tightly. Fasten securely and sew back seam. Embroider 6 (7, 7) motifs on hat, placing point X (Y, Y) on middle st.

Pompon: Wind B over a 2″ cardboard eighty times. Wind A over B eighty times. With a separate strand of yarn, tightly tie one edge; cut other side. Trim pompon and sew to top of hat.

Child's Patterned Brown and White Pullover and Hat

Sizes:

Directions are for size 3. Changes for sizes 6 and 8 are in parentheses.
Chest Size: 22″ (24″, 26″).
Finished measurements: 23″ (25½″, 28″).

Materials:

Knitting worsted-weight yarn.

Dark Brown (A)	6 (7, 8) oz.
White (B)	6 (7, 8) oz.
Bright Rose (C)	½ oz.
Orange (D)	½ oz.
Gold (E)	½ oz.
Yellow (F)	½ oz.

Size F aluminum crochet hook.
3 Small buttons.

Needles:

Sizes 6, 8, and 10, or sizes to obtain gauge.

Gauge:

Pattern st on size 10 needles: 9 sts = 2″. Stockinette st on size 8 needles: 9 sts = 2″.

Sweater

BACK:

With size 10 needles and A, cast on 53 (59, 65) sts. Attach B, leaving A at side, and begin pattern.

Row 1: With B, k 1, * sl 1 as if to purl with yarn in back, k 1; rep from * to end.

Row 2: With B, p.

Row 3: With A, k 2, * sl 1, k 1; rep from *, ending sl 1, k 2.

Row 4: With A, p. Work even until 13½″ (15½″, 17″) from beg, or desired length to back of neck, ending with Row 1 or 3 of pattern.

On next p row, bind off center 15 (17, 19) sts.

Shape Neck: Work across 19 (21, 23) sts in pattern and sl rem sts on holder. Working on one side only, dec 1 st at neck edge every other row two times. Work even on 17 (19, 21) sts until 14½″ (16½″, 18″) from beg. Bind off on p row. Work other side to correspond, reversing shaping.

FRONT:

Work as for back until 13″ (14¾″, 16¼″) from beg. Shape neck as for back. Continue to work even until front is same length as back—14½″ (16½″, 18″). Bind off on p row. Work other side to correspond, reversing shaping.

SLEEVES:

With size 8 needles and A, cast on 33 (37, 41) sts. P 1 row A. Attach B and work in st st, 2 rows B, 2 rows A. Inc 1 st each end every 1¼″ six (seven, seven) times until 45 (51, 55) sts. At the same time, when A and B stripes equal 5½″ (7″, 8″) from beg, break off A and B. Attach C. Work 4 rows each of st st with colors C, D, E, F, and B. Break off all colors except B. Attach A and starting with Row 3 of pattern st, work until 10½″ (12½″, 13¾″) from beg. Bind off on p row.

Neckband: Sew left shoulder seam. With size 6 needles, right side facing and A, pick up 56 (62, 66) sts around neck. Work in k 1, p 1 ribbing with 1 row A, 2 rows B, 2 rows A. Bind off loosely in ribbing on next row with A.

Finishing: Sew other shoulder from arm edge toward neck for *only* 1″, to allow for shoulder opening. Sew sleeves to body with center of sleeve at shoulder seam. Sew side and sleeve seams.

Edgings: On lower edge, right side facing, with F hook and color B, work 1 sc in each st. Sl st to join. End off. Attach A and work 1 sc in each sc. Sl st to join. End off. Work same edging on sleeves.

Shoulder Opening: On right front edge of shoulder opening, mark for 3 evenly spaced button loops, placing first ½" from neck edge and last ¾" from shoulder seam. Attach A to knitted neck ribbing. With F hook, sc around both sides of shoulder opening, making sure to keep work flat, and work button loops at markers as follows: ch 4, sl st in same st. Fasten off. Sew buttons opposite button loops. Weave in all ends.

Hat

With size 6 needles and A, loosely cast on 78 (84, 84) sts. Work in k 1, p 1 ribbing, with 1 row A, 2 rows B, 2 rows A, 2 rows B, 2 rows A. End off. Change to size 8 needles and work 4 rows each of st st with colors C, D, E, F, and B. Attach A and continue in st st with 2 row stripes of A and B until 5" (5½", 6") from beg. Continue stripes while shaping crown.

Dec Row 1: * K 4, k 2 tog. Rep from * across. P 1 row, k 1 row, p 1 row.

Dec Row 2: * K 3, k 2 tog. Rep from * across. P 1 row, k 1 row, p 1 row.

Dec Row 3: * K 2, k 2 tog. Rep from * across. P 1 row.

Dec Row 4: * K 1, k 2 tog. Rep from * across. P 1 row.

Dec Row 5: * K 2 tog. Rep from * across. P 1 row 13 (14, 14) sts.

Dec Row 6: K 1 (k 2, k 2), * k 3 tog. Rep from * across—5 (6, 6) sts. End off, leaving an 18" end. With a tapestry needle draw yarn through sts and pull tightly. Fasten securely and sew seam.

Pompon: Wind B over a 2" cardboard eighty times. Wind A over B eighty times. With a separate strand of yarn, tightly tie one edge; cut other side. Trim pompon and sew to top of hat.

Marianne Ake, Diamond-Patterned Mohair Pullover in Nine Colors, page 21; Rose Chenille Vest, page 4; Blue Linen Lace Pullover, page 7.

Marianne Ake, White and Gray Double-Breasted Coat with Shawl Collar, page 15; White and Green Blouson with Flowers, page 10.

Barbara Baker, Woman's Cape, page 45; Man's Alpaca V-Neck Pullover, page 33; Woman's Rainbow Popcorn Pullover, page 37.

Barbara Baker, Woman's Chenille V-Neck Pullover, page 42; Woman's
Chenille Jacket, page 30.

Dione Christensen, Chinese Jacket, page 62; Ribbon Vest, page 59; Carpet Bag, page 71.

Dione Christensen, Indian Spirit Cape, page 66; Marsden Hartley Sweater, page 52.

Phoebe Fox, Man's Beige-tone Raglan Pullover, page 87; Child's Patterned Brown and White Pullover and Hat, page 83; Striped Cowl-Neck Pullover, page 95.

Phoebe Fox, Jacket of Rainbow Stripes with Black and White Checks, page 11; Child's Cardigan and Hat with Duplicate Stitch Motifs, page 78

Maria Hart, Flower Sweater, page 102; Striped Gray Pullover, page 131;
Klee Sweater, page 107.

Maria Hart. Mohair Dress, page 125; Patchwork Coat, page 111.

Linda Mendelson, Lacy Armor Vest, page 140; Boat-Neck Sweater, page
146; Bias-Knit Geometric Vest, page 143.

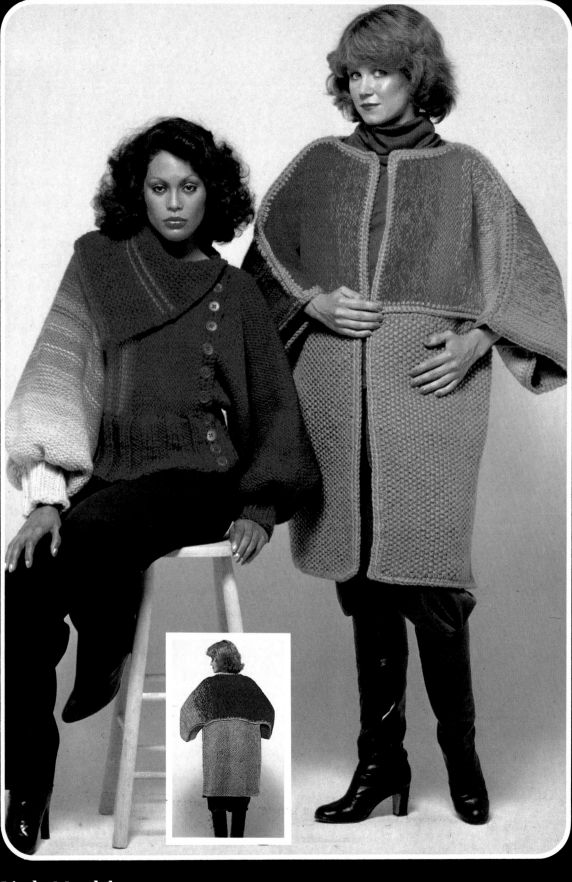

Linda Mendelson, Jacket with Big Sleeves, page 149; Rainbow Coat, page 154.

Andrée Rubin, Blue Aran Isle Poncho, page 177; Gray Shetland Cable Sweater with Saddle Shoulders, page 168; Gold Donegal Tweed Aran Isle Hooded Jacket, page 162.

Andrée Rubin, Blue and Silver Blouse with Silver Disco Bag, page 172; Off-White Shetland Lace Blouson, page 182.

Monna Weinman, Man's Crew-Neck Fair Isle Sweater, page 202; Entrelacs or Trellis Sweater, page 198.

Monna Weinman, Man's Vest, page 190; Blouse with Ruffles, page 194;
Man's Fair Isle Sweater with Turtleneck, page 202.

Man's Beige-tone
Raglan Pullover

Sizes:

Directions are for men's Small size. Changes for Medium and Large are in parentheses.
Chest Size: 38″ (40″, 41″; 43″, 44″).
Finished Measurements: 39″ (42″, 45″).

Materials:

Brushed variegated wool yarn.
   Light Beige/Gray tones (A)   12 (14, 16) oz.

Heavy-weight Donegal tweed.
   Medium Brown (B)   14 (16, 18) oz.
   Dark Brown (C)   8 (10, 12) oz.

Needles:

Size 8 straight; size 6 circular; 1 set size 6 double-pointed; or sizes to obtain given gauge.

Gauge:

Stockinette st on size 8 needles: 11 sts = 3″; 6 rows = 1″.

Note: This sweater is constructed in an unusual way, with side panels of body and sleeves worked horizontally, and back, front, and sleeve inserts worked vertically. There are no side or undersleeve seams.

BACK:

With size 8 needles and C, loosely cast on 84 (91, 98) sts. P 1 row. Continue in st st (k 1 row, p 1 row) working 4 more rows C, 6 rows B. End off C, attach 2 strands of A. With 2 strands A, k 1 row, p 1 row. Rep with B. Continue 2 row stripes until 6¾″ (7¼″, 7¾″) from beg, ending with 2 rows A. Work 6 rows st st B, then C. Bind off loosely on next row.

FRONT:

Work as for back.

SIDE PANELS:

Make 2. With size 8 needles and B, cast on 33 (35, 37) sts. P 1 row. Attach 2 strands of A, leaving B at side, and work in st st (2 rows A, 2 rows B). Inc 1 st in middle st every 1½″ (1¼″, 1″), seven (nine, eleven) times until 40 (44, 48) sts. Work even until 14¾″ (15½″, 16¼″) from beg or desired length to underarm, allowing for 2½″ ribbing. Bind off center 4 sts on p row of B.

Shape Raglan Armhole: With A, working on 18 (20, 22) sts, k 1 row, p 1 row. * With B, k across to within last 4 sts, sl 1, k 1, psso, k 2. P 1 row. With A, k 1 row, p 1 row. Rep from * seven (eight, nine) times more—10 (11, 12) sts remain. ** On next k row, work dec. P 1 row. Rep from ** dec 1 st on every k row of A and B, six (seven, eight) times more—3 sts remain. Next row: Sl 1, k 1, psso, k 1. Turn; p 2 tog. End off. Attach B and 2 strands of A to other half and work to correspond with dec shaping at beg of row (k 2, k 2 tog).

SLEEVES:

Make 2. With size 8 needles and B, cast on 28 (31, 34) sts. P 1 row. Attach 2 strands of A, leaving B at side, and work in st st (2 rows A, 2 rows B). Inc 1 st in middle st every 1″ twelve (thirteen, fourteen) times until 40 (44, 48) sts. Work even until 15½″ (16¼″, 17″) from beg or desired length to underarm, allowing for 2½″ ribbing. Bind off center 4 sts on p row of B.

Shape Raglan Cap: Work as for side panel armhole shaping.

SLEEVE INSERTS:

Make 2. With size 8 needles and C, loosely cast on 91 (98, 105) sts. P 1 row. Continue in st st with 4 more rows C, 6 rows B, 6 rows C. Bind off loosely on next row.

Finishing: Weave 4 body sections tog, with cast-on edge of back next to 1 straight edge of side panel and other straight edge of side to bound-off edge of front. Sew each raglan edge of side panels to raglan-shaped edge of sleeves. Sew sleeve inserts into sleeves, starting at wrist and continuing 1″ into top edges of front and back pieces.

Waistband: With size 6 circular needle, right side facing and C, pick up 120 (128, 136) sts from bottom edge. Work in k 1, p 1 ribbing for 6 additional rounds C, then 6 rounds B, and 6 rounds C. Loosely bind off in ribbing on next row.

Wristband: With size 6 dp needles, right side facing and C, pick up 36 (40, 44) sts evenly distributed on 3 needles. Rib as for waistband.

Neckband: With size 6 dp needles, right side facing and C, pick up 68 (72, 76) sts evenly distributed on 3 needles. Rib 6 additional rows C, 12 rows B, 6 rows C. Bind off very loosely in ribbing on next row. Turn neckband in half and loosely sew to inside sts. Weave in all ends.

Jacket of Rainbow Stripes with Black and White Checks

Sizes:

Directions are for Small sizes (6 to 8). Changes for Medium (10 to 12) and Large (14 to 16) are in parentheses.
Chest Size: 32" to 33" (34" to 35½"; 37" to 38").
Finished Measurements: 34" (36½", 39").

Materials:

Knitting worsted-weight yarn.

Red-Orange (A)	5 (6, 7) oz.
Gold (B)	5 (6, 7) oz.
Chartreuse (C)	4 (5, 6) oz.
Turquoise (D)	4 (5, 6) oz.
White (E)	9 (10, 11) oz.
Black (F)	7 (8, 9) oz.

Sizes F and G aluminum crochet hooks.

11 Black buttons, ⅜" diameter.

Needles:

Sizes 7 and 8, or sizes to obtain given gauge.

Gauge:

Stockinette st on 7 needles: 19 sts = 4"; 15 rows = 2".
Pattern st on size 8 needles: 19 sts = 4"; 19 rows = 2".

BACK:

With size 7 needles and A, cast on 71 (77, 83) sts. P 1 row. Continue in st st (k 1 row, p 1 row); working 6 additional rows A, then 8 rows each of colors B, C, and D. Fasten off. Attach E and F, and begin pattern.
Rows 1 and 2: With E, k.
Row 3: With F, k 2, * sl 1 as if to purl with yarn in back, k 2; rep from * to end.

Row 4: With F, p 2, * sl 1 as if to purl with yarn in front, p 2; rep from * to end.

Rows 5 and 6: With E, k. Rep Rows 3 through 6; eight (eight, nine) more times—38 (38, 42) rows. Fasten off. Attach A. Work 8 rows each of st st with colors A, B, C, and D. Break off. Attach E and F and work pattern st as before.break off. Attach A and work 8 rows each of st st with A and B. On last p row of B, bind off center 27 sts. Fasten off. Attach C.

Shape Neck: Work across 22 (25, 28) sts in st st for 8 rows each with colors C and D. Bind off loosely on next row with D. Attach C to other side of neck and work to correspond.

LEFT FRONT:

With size 7 needles and A, cast on 35 (38, 41) sts and work as for back. Bind off first 13 sts on last p row of color B of third striped section. Attach C and complete neck on 22 (25, 28) sts as for back.

RIGHT FRONT:

Work to correspond to left front, reversing neck shaping by binding off the last 13 sts on last p row of B of third striped section. Complete neck as for back.

FRONT INSERT:

With size 7 needles and A, cast on 20 sts. Work as for back. Bind off on last p row of color B of third striped section.

SLEEVES:

With size 7 needles and A, cast on 77 (80, 83) sts. Work as for back, completing 8 rows of color A (B-B) of the third striped section. Bind off loosely on next row.

HOOD:

With size 7 needles and A, cast on 149 (152, 155) sts. Work striped (32 rows) and patterned (38 rows) areas as for back. With F, k 1 row. Bind off in knitting on next row. Fold in half; sew back seam.

Crocheted Edging:

Round 1: With G hook, right side facing and color E, sl st around each piece. Make sure that work lies flat and corresponding edges have the same number of sts. Sl st to join. End off.

Round 2: With F hook and E, work 1 sc in each sl st and 3 sc in corner sts to turn. Sl st to join. End off.

Round 3: (for all pieces except front insert): With F hook and color F, rep Rnd 2.

Round 3 (for front insert *only*): On left side edge, mark for 11 evenly spaced button loops, placing first loop 4″ from lower edge and last loop at the top of insert. With F hook and E, work 1 rnd of sc along all edges with 3 sc in corner sts to turn, and button loops at markers. Button loop: Ch 4, sl st in same st. Sl st to join. Fasten off.

Finishing: Sew shoulder seams. Sew sleeve seams. Fold armhole edge of sleeve in half with seam at top; sew to body. Sew side seams, leaving a 4″ opening at each lower edge for side slits. Sew right side of front insert to front edge, leaving a 4″ opening at lower edge for slit. Sew buttons to front edge opposite button loops. Placing back seam of hood at center back of neck, sew hood to neck edge. (Front edge of hood will be approx 2½″ in from front neck edges.) Secure all ends.

Tassels: Make 2 with colors A, B, C, and D. Wind yarn over a 2″ cardboard fifteen times. Tie ends tog with a 12″ chain or twisted cord of F at top of cardboard. Remove cardboard. Holding all tassel strands tog, tightly wrap tassel color yarn around tassel; knot securely. Weave in all ends behind wrapping. Trim tassel. Fasten cord of tassel D to top of crochet edge of each front piece, not insert. Attach 1 C tassel on each side 1½″ below. Rep with B and A tassels.

Striped Cowl-Neck Pullover

Sizes:

Directions are for Small size (6 to 8). Changes for Medium (10 to 12) and Large (14 to 16) are in parentheses.
Chest Size: 31″ to 32½″ (34″ to 35½″; 37″ to 38½″).
Finished Measurements: 33″ (36″, 39″).

Materials:

Knitting worsted-weight yarn.
Black (A)	11 (11, 12) oz.

Light-weight mohair loop.
Black (B)	7 (7, 8) oz.

Medium-weight wool novelty loop.
Rust (C)	12 (12, 13) oz.
White (D)	5 (5, 6) oz.

Heavy-weight wool novelty loop.
Bright Pink (E)	2 (2, 2) oz.
Dark Orange (F)	2 (2, 2) oz.

Knitting worsted.
Wine (G)	2 (3, 3) oz.
Magenta (F)	3 (3, 4) oz.

Note: Single strands of knitting worsted may be substituted for the suggested novelty yarns if you adjust needle size to achieve the same gauge.

Needles:

Size 7, or size to obtain gauge.

Gauge:

Garter rib st on size 7 needles: 9 sts = 2″; 8 rows = 1″.

Note: This sweater is worked vertically by starting at side edge and working back and forth from shoulder to lower edge.

BACK:

Beg at side edge with 1 strand of A and B tog, and cast on 110 (115, 120) sts. P 1 row. Attach 2 strands of C, leaving A and B at side, and beg garter rib pattern.

Rows 1 and 2: With 2 strands tog of C, k 2 rows.

Row 3: With 1 strand each of A and B, k.

Row 4: With 1 strand each of A and B, p. Work in pattern until 2¼″ (2¾″, 3¼″) from beg, ending with Row 4 of pattern. Fasten off and begin decorative stripes. With E, k 2 rows. With F, k 2 rows. With G, * k 1 row, p 1 row; rep from * with H, G, H, G. With F, k 2 rows. With E, k 2 rows. Fasten off. Attach 1 strand each of A and B, k 1 row. P 1 row, binding off last 5 sts. Attach 2 strands of D and work in garter rib st on 105 (110, 115) sts until 8″ (9″, 9½″) from beg of sweater. Fasten off D, attach 2 strands C. Continue in garter rib until 11½″ (12½″, 13½″) from beg of sweater. Cast on 5 sts at neck edge and continue in pattern until left shoulder is the same length as the right shoulder, ending with Row 4. Bind off on next row.

FRONT:

Begin at side edge with 1 strand of A and B tog, cast on 110 (115, 120) sts. Work garter rib and decorative stripes as for back until 4¾″ (5¼″, 5¾″) from beg. End off. Attach 1 strand of A and B, and k 1 row. Bind off 10 sts at beg of p row. Attach 2 strands D and work garter rib as for back. Fasten off D. Attach 2 strands C and continue in pattern until 11½″ (12½″, 13½″) from beg. Cast on 10 sts at neck edge and complete shoulder as for back.

SLEEVES:

With size 7 needles and 1 strand A and B tog, cast on 31 (32, 34) sts. P 1 row. Attach 2 strands of D and work in garter rib until 2″ from beg. Inc 1 st between every st across row—61 (63, 67) sts. Continue in same colors until 2¾″ from beg. End off. Attach E and beg decorative stripes. At same time, when work measures 4″ from beg, and every 1¾″ (2″, 2″) thereafter, inc 1 st each side until 75 (77, 81) sts. After decorative stripes, work

garter rib with 1 strand of A and B, and 2 strands of C until sleeve measures 18½″ (19″, 19½″) from beg or desired length to underarm. Bind off on Row 2.

COLLAR:

With size 7 needles and 1 strand of A and B tog, cast on 88 (92, 96) sts. P 1 row. Attach 2 strands of C and work in garter rib, as for back, until 4¼″ (4¾″, 4¾″) from beg, ending with Row 4. Fasten off. Attach E and work decorative stripes. At same time, when work measures 6½″ (7″, 7″) inc 4 evenly spaced sts. After decorative stripes, work garter rib with 1 strand of A and B tog, and 2 strands of D. Inc 4 evenly spaced sts when collar measures 7½″ (8″, 8″) from beg, and again at 8½″ (9″, 9″) from beg. Continue in pattern until 9½″ (10″, 10″) from beg. Loosely bind off on Row 2 of pattern.

Finishing: Sew or weave shoulder seams. Fold sleeves in half lengthwise to find midpoint. Sew sleeves to body so that midpoint is at shoulder seam. Sew side and undersleeve seams. Sew collar seam to form tube. Sew wrong side of cowl collar to right side of body, so that when the collar is folded outward, its right side will be facing the right side of the garment. Weave in all ends.

Maria Hart

Maria Hart graduated from the Philadelphia College of Art with a B.A. in fashion design, received further training from the Philadelphia Textile Institute, took additional courses at the Haystack Mountain School of Crafts in Maine, and studied textiles with Jack Lenor Larson and painting with Will Barnet. With such an amazing array of craft and art skills—dyeing, weaving, knitting, crochet, embroidery, painting, and needlepoint, to name a few—it is hardly surprising that her designs are an art form in their own right. Freeing her work from conventional restrictions, Maria combines unusual materials with a truly innovative sense of style and creates exciting designs already familiar to the thousands of readers of Ladies' Home Journal Needle & Craft and Simplicity.

"I specialize in doing things that appear to be complicated but aren't really all that difficult to do: The designing may be fairly taxing but the actual making of the project is not. The big patchwork and quilted coat, for example, looks like the kind of thing that would take a year and a day to put together, but it's just strips of knitting. If a person knits one strip or a fairly simple section each day, the whole thing shouldn't take more than twenty or thirty days to complete. This coat is typical of my work in that a person with the desire and the wherewithal can easily change any part of it—by adding to it or taking away or changing the strips—to make it a very personal statement. The same thing is true of the sweater with the flower pot and flowers on the front. Its knit-in design is embellished with a lot of embroidery, but how much embroidery you want to do is optional—more, less, or none at all.

"I'm a firm believer in mixing techniques; I'll try anything. I've taken old lace doilies with figurative designs in them and painted them to look very real. I'll take a needlepoint that I started and never finished and I'll appliqué it to something else, maybe to some knitting; I won't know whether two unusual things will work together unless I try it. There are no rules—at least, I don't know who's enforcing them if there are any. That's the attitude I feel everyone should have."

Maria Hart

Flower Sweater

This sweater has a short, rolled sleeve, tunic top with the look of Irish smocking at the neck, and accents of Polish embroidery. There are side pockets at the hips and a three-button closing on the shoulder.

The design may be entirely knitted in, or partially done and completed in duplicate stitch. If duplicate stitch is used, best results will be obtained if the pot is knitted in. Work from graph to Pale Yellow section, complete pot in Pale Yellow and then work duplicate stitch to complete pot, flowers, and details.

Size:

One size fits all.

Materials:

7 4-oz. skeins worsted-weight yarn in Olive.
Use 1 skein less if design is knitted in.
Small amounts of similar weight yarns in the following colors:

Olive (A)	Dark Gold (N)
White (B)	Gold (P)
Purple (C)	Pale Pink (Q)
Blue (D)	Pale Orange (R)
Red (E)	Mint Green (O)
Pink (F)	Medium Pink (S)
Burgundy (G)	Pale Yellow (T)
Lilac (H)	Pale Green (U)
Yellow (I)	Dark Yellow (V)
Pale Lavender (J)	Cream (W)
Moss Green (K)	Lavender (X)
Green (L)	Rose (Y)
Dark Green (M)	Pale Blue (Z)

Small amounts of 3-ply needlepoint yarn, used singly.
¼ yd. Lightweight wool jersey for pocket lining.
3 Small buttons.

Hook:

Size G aluminum crochet.

Needles:

Sizes 5 and 8, or sizes to obtain gauge.

Gauge:

4 sts = 1″, 6 rows = 1″.

FRONT:

With Olive and size 5 needles, cast on 80 sts. Work in k 1, p 1 ribbing for 2″.

Next row: Work in ribbing for 28 sts, k 24, work in ribbing for rem 28 sts.

Next row: Work in ribbing for 28 sts, p 24, work in ribbing for rem 28 sts.

Next row: Begin with Row 1 of graph (rib 28, k 3 Olive, k 18 White, k 3 Olive, rib 28).

Work, following graph and keeping first and last 28 sts in ribbing until 3½″ from beg. Beg st st.

Next row: K across working 8 inc each side by (inc 1, k 4) 7 times, end inc 1—96 sts.

Change to size 8 needles.

Continue in st st following graph for design and, at the same time, inc 1 st each side every other row twice—100 sts. Work for 15″ or 90 rows to armhole.

ARMHOLE:

Cast off 7 sts at beg of next 2 rows. Beg center panel and armhole dec on next row, k 1, k 2 tog, k 16, Row 1 of pattern sts on next 48 sts, k 17, sl 1, psso, k 1.

Next row: P 18, work Row 2 of pattern, p 18.

Continue in this way repeating 4 rows of pattern on center 48 sts and dec 1 st each side every other row seven more times—70 sts. Work until 8″ from armhole.

Pattern Stitch:

Row 1: * (K 1, p 1, k 1) in first st. Rep from * eleven times—48 pattern sts.

Row 2: Purl.

Row 3: * P 3 tog, (k 1, p 1, k 1) in next st. Rep from * eleven times.

Row 4: Purl.

NECK:

Work across 28 sts, cast off 14 sts, work across last 28 sts. Working on these last 28 sts, p 1 row. Dec 1 st at neck edge every other row six times. At the same time, when front is 2″ from neck, cast off sts, beg dec for shoulder. Cast off 6 sts twice, 7 sts once. End off. Work other side to correspond.

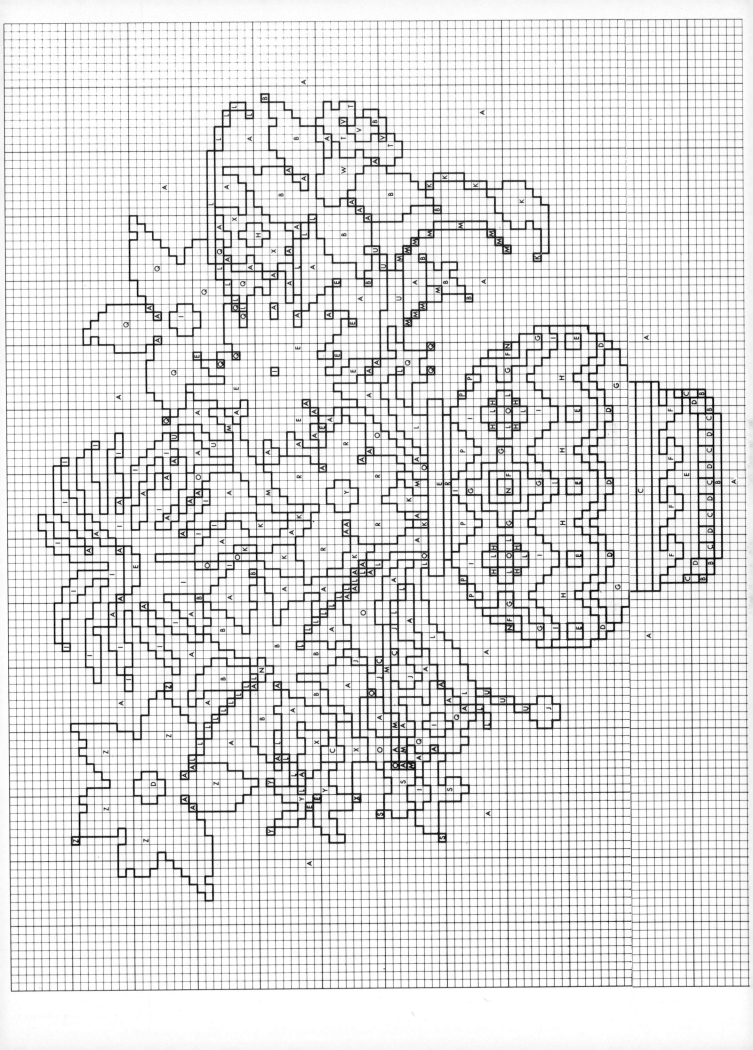

BACK:

With Olive and size 5 needles, cast on 80 sts. Work in k 1, p 1 ribbing for 3½". Beg st st. On first row inc 16 sts by working inc 1, k 4 across row. Change to size 8 needles. Inc 1 st each side every other row twice—100 sts. Work even until 15" from beg, or to match front.

Armholes: Cast off 7 sts at beg of next 2 rows, then dec 1 st each side every other row eight times—70 sts. Work as for front until same length to shoulder. Cast off 6 sts at beg of next 4 rows, then 7 sts at beg of next 2 rows. End off.

SLEEVES:

With Olive and size 5 needles, cast on 50 sts. Work in k 1, p 1 ribbing for 3¾". Beg st st. On first row inc 24 sts by k 2, inc 1 across row, ending k 2, 74 sts. Change to size 8 needles. P 1 row.
Work 2 rows in st st, then inc 1 st each side every 4th row six times—80 sts. Work even for 8 rows.

Cap: Cast off 7 sts at beg of next 2 rows. On next row, dec 1 st each side, then every 4th row five times—54 sts. Dec 1 st each side every other row six times—42 sts. Bind off 2 sts at beg of next 10 rows. Bind off rem 22 sts.

Inside pocket panels: With Olive and size 8 needles, cast on 6 sts. Work in st st for 6½". Bind off all sts.

Finishing: Complete front design. Work in all yarn ends. Follow picture for satin and chain st embroidery or work as desired for flower centers and details. Sew sweater side seams leaving a 6" opening above ribbing for pockets. Sew pocket panels to sweater back above ribbing. With Olive and size G crochet hook, work 1 row sc on sweater front opening. On wrong side, cut lining to fit and stitch to inside edge of packet panels and along top and bottom to sweater front. Sew right shoulder seam. Sew left shoulder to beginning of pattern from armhole. With Olive and size G crochet hook work 1 row sc around shoulder and neck opening. On front shoulder, evenly space 3 loops by working ch 3, sk 1 sp, sc in next sp. Sew on buttons to match loops. Sew sleeve seams and set in sleeves. Block lightly.

Klee Sweater

Size:

One size fits all.

Materials:

Lightweight mohair, 2-oz. skeins, 1 each in
    Pink
    Pale Blue
    Dark Blue

Standard-weight mohair, 125-yd. skeins, 1 each in
    Black
    Light Gold
    Olive
    Orange

Chenille, 1 skein.

Pale Moss, or substitute 1 skein Light Gold mohair.

Hook:

Size G aluminum crochet.

Needles:

Sizes 8 and 15, or sizes to obtain gauge.

Gauge:

On size 15 needles, approx 2½ sts = 1″, 3 rows = 1″.
This sweater is worked on large needles from the neck edge to the hem. Insets form the shoulders. After knitting, the body of the sweater is dyed with a quick tint of Aqua dye, which gives the sweater a muted look. The ribbing is then attached, the neck edge crocheted, and true color patches applied.

Back and front are the same.

With Pink and size 15 needles, cast on 62 sts. Work in garter st for 5″. End on odd row. P 1 row.

Att Olive and k 1 row.

Att Black and work in garter st for 3½″. For sleeve, cast off 7 sts at beg of next 2 rows—48 sts.

Att Pink, k front, p back for 4 rows.

Att Olive, k front, p back for 4 rows.

Att Light Gold, p front, k back for 4 rows.

Att Black, k front, p back for 4 rows.

Att Orange, k in garter st for 3 rows.

Att Pink, k 2 rows. Cast off.

RIBBING:

With Dark Blue and size 8 needles, cast on 122 sts. Work in ribbing (k 2, p 2, end k 2) for 1½″. Continue in ribbing adding 1 row Pale Blue, 1 row Dark Blue, 2 rows Pale Blue, 2 rows Dark Blue, 3 rows Pale Blue and 4 rows Black. Bind off.

SHOULDER INSETS:

With Pink and size 15 needles, cast on 10 sts. Work in garter st. Dec 1 st each side every other row to 2 sts. K 2 tog. End off.

APPLIQUÉS:

Breast pocket: With Pink and size 8 needles, cast on 15 sts. Work in st st for 8 rows. Att Pale Moss chenille and continue in st st for 8 rows. Bind off. Rib side is right side.

Center stripe: With Orange and size 8 needles, cast on 8 sts. Work in pattern of p 2, k 4, p 2 for 10 rows. Continue 10 row patterns with Pale Moss chenille, Dark Blue, Pale Blue, Pink, Black, Olive Green, and Light Gold. Bind off.

Small triangle: With Orange and size 8 needles, cast on 13 sts. P 1 row. Dec 1 st each side every other row to 3 sts. Dec 1 st, turn, work 2 sts, k 2 tog. End off.

Large triangle: With Light Gold and size 8 needles, cast on 20 sts. P one row. Work in st st, dec 1 st on one side every other row to end.

Dyeing sweater: Use ½ package of Aqua dye according to directions. Let water cool. Immerse sweater for 10 to 15 minutes. Rinse in cold water until excess dye is removed and rinse water is clear. Remember, we don't want it to be dark, only tinted. Roll in a towel to remove excess water and let dry.

Finishing: Sew side seams. Sew in shoulder insets having point of inset about 1″ from armhole edge. Sew ribbing band. Ease sweater evenly to ribbing band. With G crochet hook, sl st together. Check diameter. It should be wide enough for sweater to slip on easily, but small enough for sl st joining to rest on hips.

Attach pockets and front band with tapestry needle and matching yarn.

Shell neck edge: With G crochet hook and Pale Blue, beg ½″ from join on inset piece. Sc in first st, * sk 1 st, 5 dc in next st, sk 1 st, sc in next st. Rep from * around.

There should be 19 shells. Join with sl st. Break off Pale Blue, att Dark Blue, working 5 dc in sc of previous row and sc in third dc of Pale Blue shell—19 shells. End off. Steam lightly.

Patchwork Coat

Patchwork design is worked in vertical panels approximately 23″ in length and joined with contrasting strips. Sleeves, collar, and shoulder yokes are worked in geometric pieces and joined to coat, which is then lined and quilted. Mix yarns and colors as desired.

Note: Some sections, because of their complexity, are illustrated. Substitute stitches from *Mon Tricot* or other knitting dictionaries wherever desired.

Size:

One size fits all.

Materials:

Approx 4 ½ lbs. worsted-weight yarn in a wide variety of colors. Scraps of yarn work well. Combine yarns to give same gauge.
1 3-Yd. piece ofpolyester batting in sheet form.
2 Yds. thin wool knit for lining (approx 29″ to 30 ″ wide in tube).
10 Black snaps for closing, matching thread.
Burgundy grosgrain ribbon to line front strips.

Hook:

Size D aluminum crochet.

Needles:

Sizes 7 and 8; one size 8 dp. Stitch holder, tapestry needle.

Gauge:

4 sts = 1″, 5 rows = 1″.

COAT BODY:

Joining strips, make a total of 8. Use size 8 needles.

#1: Purple cable.
  With size 8 needles, cast on 8 sts.
Rows 1 and 3: P 2, k 4, p 2.
Rows 2 and 4: K 2, p 4, k 2.
Row 5: P 2, sl next 2 sts onto dp needle and leave at front of work, k 2 sts, k 2 sts from dp needle, p 2.
Row 6: As Row 2. Work till 23″ high, approx 24 twists, ending with Row 4. Cast off.

#2: Burgundy and Red strip:
  Cast on 6 sts in Burgundy.
Row 1: P across.
Row 2: K across.
Row 3: P 2 Burgundy, p 2 Red, p 2 Burgundy.
Rows 4 through 8: Rep Row 3. Rep these 8 rows until 23″ high, approx 15 Red checks. End with Row 2.

#3: Blue tweed strip.
  Cast on 6 sts.
  P for 2″ on front side.
  K for 2″ on front side. Continue in blocks of alternating k and p rows until approx 23″. Cast off.

#4: Magenta mohair strip.
  Cast on 6 sts.
Row 1: P 2, k 2, p 2.
Row 2: K 2, p 2, k 2. Work until 23″ high. Cast off.

#5: Pale Yellow.
  Cast on 6 sts.
  Work in seed st for 23″.
Row 1: K 1, p 1, k 1, p 1, k 1, p 1.
Row 2: P 1, k 1, p 1, k 1, p 1, k 1.
  With contrasting yarn and duplicate st follow picture to stitch design at bottom of strip.

#6: Red Orange and Green strip.
  Cast on 7 sts in Green.
Row 1, back: P across.
Row 2, front: K 1, Green, k 2 Orange, k 1 Green, k 2 Orange, k 1 Green.
Row 3, back: P 1 Green, k 2 Orange, p 1 Green, k 2 Orange, p 1 Green.
Row 4, front: K 1 Green, p 2 Orange, k 1 Green, p 2 Orange, k 1 Green.
Row 5, back: P 1 Green, k 2 Orange, p 1 Green, k 2 Orange, p 1 Green.
Row 6, front: K in Green across.
  Continue in pattern until 23″. Cast off.

#7 and 8: Front of coat.

  Note: A finer Burgundy yarn is used to avoid bulkiness.
  With size 7 needles, cast on 8 sts.

Row 1: * P across.

Row 2, front: K 1, left cross on next 2 sts (insert right-hand needle into the front of 2nd st on left needle, k, then k first st on same needle, drop off). K rem 5 sts.

Row 3 and all alt rows: P across.

Rows 4, 6, and 8: K across. Rep from * for cable.
Work until approx 34″ long.

PATCHWORK PANELS:

With size 8 needles, beg at lower edge of first panel on right side. Cast on 25 sts.

Panel #1: Right side front.

Block #1:

A brick pattern worked in Pale Yellow and Green.

Row 1: P across in Green.

Row 2: K 1 Green, * k 2 Yellow, k 1 Green. Rep from * across.

Row 3: P 1 Green, * k 2 Yellow, p 1 Green. Rep from * across.

Row 4: K 1 Green, * p 2 Yellow, k 1 Green. Rep from * across.
Rep Rows 1 through 4 four more times, end with a p 1 row.

Block #2: Cable.

Row 1: Inc 1 st to 26 sts and work across in p 1, (k 4, p 1). Work in classic cable pattern forming cable on k 4 sts every 4 rows. Work for approx 4½″.

Block #3: Diagonal.

Dec 1 st to 25 sts.

Row 1: K 1 Pink * k 2 Burgundy, k 2 Pink. Rep from * across.
Work Row 2 to correspond to color sequence. On Row 3 beg forming diagonal to right. Change colors every 2 rows for approx 4″.

Block #4: Vertical stripe.

Work in st st having 8 vertical stripes. There will be 3 sts in Dark Green alternating with 2 sts Light Green across row. Work for approx 4½″.

Block #5: Argyle.

Row 1: K 1 Yellow, * k 5 Orange, k 1 Yellow, Rep from * across.

Row 2: P 1 Yellow, * p 5 Orange, p 1 Yellow. Rep from * across.
Beg Argyle pattern having both a k and a p row between each st change. Work until entire length of piece is 23″.

Panel #2: Front. With size 8 needles, cast on 25 sts.

Block #1: Diagonal.

With 2 colors, work diagonal stripe the same as in Block #3 of first panel. Work for approx 3½″.

Block #2: Horizontal stripe:

Work horizontal stripes as follows: with dark color, k 2 rows; with light color, k 1 row, p 1 row. Rep these 4 rows five times more.

Block #3: Jacquard.

Work in jacquard pattern for 4½″.

Block #4: Blue diamond.

Follow chart.

Block #5:

Work in chessboard stitch for 3½″.

Block #6:

Key design in st st.

Row 1: K across with * 5 sts Gray, 5 Magenta. Rep from * once, end 5 Gray.

Row 3: P in color sequence.

Rows 2 and 4: * K 1 Gray, k 3 Magenta, k 1 Gray, k 5 Magenta. Rep from * once, end k 3 Magenta, k 1 Gray.

Row 5: K 1 Gray, * k 3 Magenta, k 7 Gray. Rep from * once, end k 3 Magenta, k 1 Gray.

Row 6: K across in Magenta.

Row 7: P across in Magenta.

Repeat these 7 rows three more times. Work in st st in Magenta to 23″ from beg of piece.

Panel #3: Back, With size 8 needles, cast on 25 sts.

Block #1: Work in reverse st st to have all p on right side.

Row 1: P across.

Row 2: K 5 Lilac, * k 5 Burgundy, k 5 Lilac. Rep from * twice.

Row 3: P 5 Burgundy, * p 5 Lilac, p 5 Burgundy. Rep from * twice.

Rows 4 and 6: K 5 Lilac, * k 5 Burgundy, k 5 Lilac. Rep from * twice.

Rows 5 and 7: P 5 Lilac, * k 5 Burgundy, p 5 Lilac. Rep from * twice.

Row 8: K 5 Burgundy, * k 5 Lilac, k 5 Burgundy. Rep from * twice. Rep these 8 rows twice.

Block #2: Chevrons. Work in st st.

Row 1: Work across alternating 5 sts in MC and CC.

Row 2: Work 1 st in CC, 3 in MC, 1 in CC, alternating colors every 5 sts.

Row 3: Work 2 sts in CC, 1 in MC, 2 in CC again alternating every 5 sts.

Reverse colors and work until there are 5 chevrons.

Block #3: Brick.

Work as for Block #1 in panel #1. Work only 3 brick sections having Yellow sts in middle brick section in p, not st st.

Block #4: Work across in k 2, p 2 ribbing having 1 extra k 1 at end.

Work 2 more rows in ribbing.

Next row: P 2 Black, k 2 Red across, end k 1 Black.

Next row: P 1 Black, p 2 Red, p 2 Black across.

Work 6 rows in Black ribbing.

Repeat Red rows.

Work 3 rows in Black ribbing.

Block #5: Work in pennant pattern for 3″.

Block #6: Follow chart.

Block #7: Zigzag.

Follow chart. Work until entire piece is 23″.

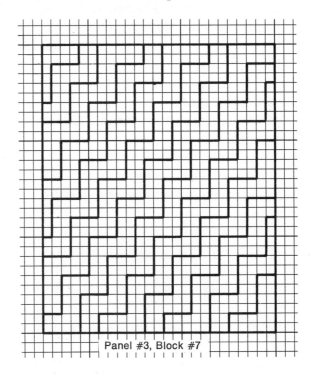

Panel #3, Block #7

Panel #4: Center Back. With size 8 needles cast on 26 sts.

Block #1: Cable.

Work in snaky cable for 4″.

Block #2: Two-toned cable.

Row 1: * P 4 Beige, k 2 Green. Rep from * three times, end p 2 Beige.

Row 2: K 2 Beige, * p 2 Green, k 4 Beige. Rep from * three times.

Row 3: P 3 Beige, * cable 2 Green, p 4 Beige. Rep from * across.

Continue cable every 2 rows, moving 1 st to the right three more times. Then cable left five times. Cable right five times.

Block #3: Dec 1 st for chessboard pattern.

Work in chessboard pattern for 3 sections, approx 3¼″.

Block #4:

In same colors work in brick pattern having 1 st in brick and 1 st in outline. Work 2 rows for brick centers. Work for 4 brick sections.

Block #5: Jacquard.

Work in same jacquard pattern as in Block #3 in Panel #2, for 4″.

Block #6:

Follow chart for design.

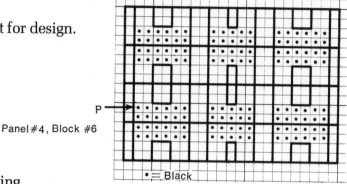

Panel #4, Block #6

• = Black

Block #7: Grating.

Work in grating stitch until entire piece measures 23″ from beg.

Panel #5: Left Back, with size 8 needles, cast on 25 sts.

Block #1: Worked as Block 7 of Panel #3 with colors and zigzag reversed. Work for 20 rows.

Block #2: Inc 1 st to 26 sts. Work as cable pattern in block #2 of first panel, but have cable every 6 rows. Work for 4½″, approx 5 cables.

Block #3: Work in block pattern alternating every 3 rows with 2 sts in White and Black. For variation, p White, k Black.

Block #4: Work in 2 colors, 2 sts each forming zigzag to right with 2 rows between changes.

Block #5: Knit, with same colors, 2 sections of the jacquard pattern from block #3, panel #2.

Block #6: Square Bull's Eye.

Work 4 rows st st in Pale Yellow. Work next 4 rows in 4 Pale Yellow, p 17 Red, 4 Pale Yellow. Red sts are all p on right side. Next 3 rows are 4 sts Pale Yellow, 4 sts Red, 9 sts Pink in st st, 4 sts Red, 4 sts Pale Yellow. On next 2 rows have 3 center sts, p on front in Green. Reverse to complete block.

Block #7: Worked in k 3 rows, p 3 rows. Change color every 3 rows having bands of Gold, Blue, Orange, Black, Lilac, Magenta and Dark Green. Work extra rows, if necessary, until 23″ from beg.

Panel #6: Left Side, with size 8 needles, cast on 25 sts.

Block #1: Work in garter st for 3″.

Block #2: Work zigzag in 3 colors, 2 sts each, changing 1 st each row five times to left, then five times to the right. Rep once.

Block #3:

Row 1: (P 1, k 1, p 1, k 1, p 1, k 5) twice, end with p 1, k 1, p 1, k 1, p 1.

Row 2: K on p, p on k.

Rows 3 and 4: Rep Rows 1 and 2.

Row 5: Reverse block beg with k 5.

Work second section of 8 rows, then rows 1 through 4 once.

Block #4: Follow graph.

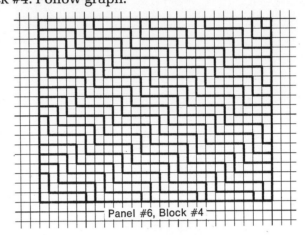

Panel #6, Block #4

Block #5: Rep block #3 having p sts in Black, k sts in Red.

Block #6: Work in ribbing of k 5, p 5 for 3".

Block #7: Work in seed st until 23" from beg.

Panel #7: Left side front, with size 8 needles, cast on 25 sts.

Block #1: Follow graph.

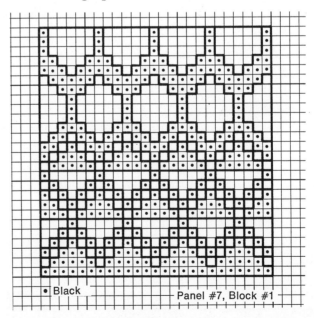

• Black   Panel #7, Block #1

Block #2: Work first 8 and last 9 sts in seed st. Work cable on center (p 2, k 4, p 2) sts every 6th row, three times.

Block #3: Work in checker board pattern in 2 colors in 2 sts each. Work 2 rows before changing. Work for 20 rows.

118

Block #4: Work in grating pattern for 3½″.
Block #5: K 1 row p 5 rows four times, k 5 rows.
Block #6: Follow graph.

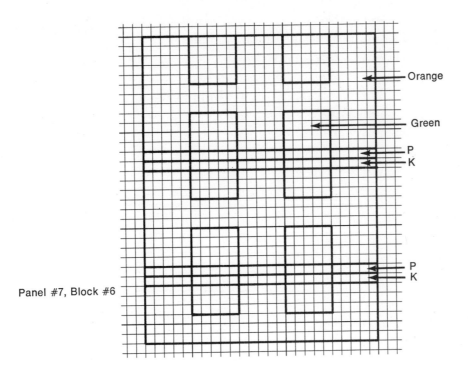

Panel #7, Block #6

RIGHT FRONT SHOULDER SECTION:

With size 8 needles and Burgundy, cast on 33 sts. K 1 row. Work 3 sections of jacquard pattern in Burgundy and Blue. Change to Blue-Gray tweed and work in ribbing of k 5, p 5, having k 3 on last sts. Work for 10 rows. Work 4 sections of horizontal stripes. P 3 rows Black, k 3 rows Moss Green. Rep once. With Lilac and Burgundy work zigzag to left, changing every 3 rows. Begin brick pattern as for Block #1 in Panel #1. On 9th row of brick pattern, cast off 14 sts for neck. Finish shoulder section in ribbing in k 2, p 2. At the same time, dec 1 st at neck edge every other row five times. Bind off rem sts. See graph.

LEFT FRONT SHOULDER SECTION:

Follow graph, and work neck dec to correspond to right side.

BACK SECTION:

With size 8 needles and Burgundy, cast on 66 sts. Work as for right front shoulder section to end of brick pattern. Then work in Argyle pattern (k 1 Yellow, k 5 Gold) changing pattern every row. Work for 2″. Bind off 14 st at beg of next 2 rows. Place rem 38 sts on holder.

119

SLEEVES, TOP SECTION:

For each sleeve, with size 8 needles, cast on 37 sts.

Right sleeve: Follow graph for sts.
Section 1: Seed st.
Section 2: Work as Block #2, Panel #3.
Section 3: Brick pattern.
Section 4: 2 St, 2 color zigzag to right.
Section 5: Argyle, worked as upper back.
Section 6: Snaky cable.
Section 7: P on front.
Section 8: P 2, k 2 ribbing.
Section 9: Follow chart.

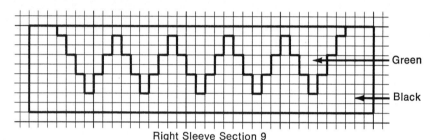

Green

Black

Right Sleeve Section 9

Section 10: Seed st for 8 rows.
Section 11: P on front for 8 rows.

Left Sleeve: Sections remain the same, sts change.
Section 1: Seed st.
Section 2: Work as Block #1, Panel #2.
Section 3: Garter st.
Section 4: Work as block #2, Panel #2.
Section 5: Work in k 1, p 1 ribbing.
Section 6: Work as block #1, Panel #5.
Section 7: Seed st.
Section 8: K 2, p 2 ribbing.
Section 9: Work in trellis st to end (no sections 10 and 11. Section 9 covers all.)

SHOULDER PANELS:

Make 2. With size 8 needles, cast on 25 sts, wrong side. K 1, p 4, k 1, (p 1, k 1, p 1,) across the next 13 sts ending k 1, p 4, k 1.
Next row, right side: P 1, sl 1 k sts on dp needle, hold in back of work, k next 2 sts, k 2 sts from dpn, cable made p 1, k 1, p 1, over next 13 sts, rep cable.

Note: Cables will be made every 7th row.

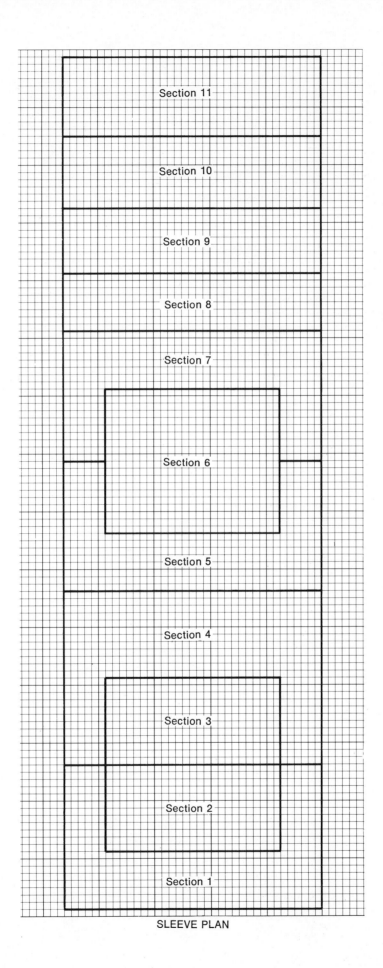

SLEEVE PLAN

121

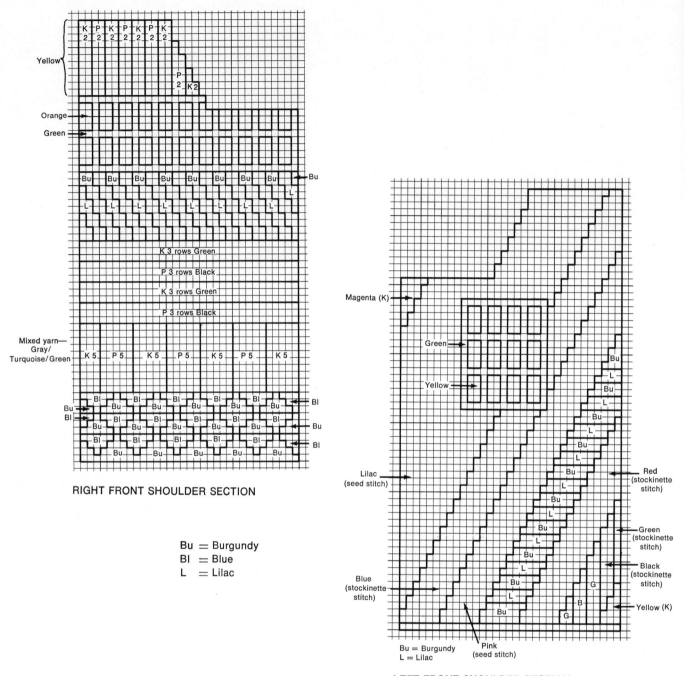

RIGHT FRONT SHOULDER SECTION

Bu = Burgundy
Bl = Blue
L = Lilac

LEFT FRONT SHOULDER SECTION

Bu = Burgundy
L = Lilac

There are 3 cables, four twist rows, with seed pattern in between. On 4th cable, change pattern.

Next row: P 1, work cable, (p 1, k 4, p 1,) will be new cable k 1, p 1, k 1, seed st center, (p 1, k 4, p 1,) for new cable, make cable, p 1, right side.

Next row, back: K 1, p 4, k 1, p 4, k 1 (k 1, p 1, k 1, seed st k 1, p 4, k 1, p 4, k 1.

Next row, front: K 1, p 1, k 1, p 1, k 1, p 1, cable next 4 sts, p 1, (k
1, p 1, k 1,) p 1, cable on 4 sts, p 1, k 1, p 1, k 1, p 1, k 1.
Continue up to 4th cable row, p 1, k 4, p 1, cable 4 sts, p 1, etc.

Note: There are 2 purls on the front near the cable and on the
back k 1, p 1, when starting into seed st.
There are 7 blocks on this strip ending with the cable at the
edge as originally started. Cast off on front side.

UNDERSLEEVES:

With size 8 needles, cast on 37 sts.
Row 1, wrong side: K 1, p 4, k 1, work in ribbing, up to last 6 sts,
then k 1, p 4, k 1.
Row 2, right side: P 1, cable 4, p 1, work ribbing to 6th st then p
2, cable 4, p 1. Continue for 2½″, then keeping cables, change
ribbing to seed st. Continue until you have cabled nineteen
times. After 19th cable, on back row, k across. Cast off on front
side.

BLUE COLLAR:

With size 8 needles, and Blue yarn cast on 10 sts.
Row 1, back: K 1, p 2, k 7.
Row 2, front: P 6, sl 1 to dp needle, hold in back of work, k next
2 sts, p 1 from dpn, p 1.
Row 3: K 2, p 2, k 6.
Row 4: P 5, sl 1 to dpn, hold in back of work, k 2, p st from
needle, p 2.
Row 5: K 3, p 2, k 5.
Row 6: P 4, sl 1 st to dpn, hold in back of work, k 2, p st from
dpn, p 3.
Row 7: K 4, p 2, k 4.
Row 8: P 3, sl 1 st to dpn, same as above, k 2, p st from dpn, p 4.
Row 9: K 5, p 2, k 3.
Row 10: P 2, sl 1 st to dpn, same as above, k 2, p st from dpn, p 4.
Row 11: K 6, p 2, p 2.
Row 12: P 1, sl 1 st to dpn, same as above k 2, p st from dpn, p 6.
Row 13: K 7, p 2, p 1.
Row 14: P 1, sl next 2 k sts to dpn, hold in front of work, p 1, k 2
from dpn, p 6.
Row 15: K 2, p 2, k 6.
Row 16: P 2, sl next 2 k sts to dpn, hold in front, p next st, k 2
from dpn, p 5.
Row 17: K 3, p 2, k 5.
Row 18: P 3, sl 2 k sts to dpn, hold in front of work, p next st, k 2
from dpn, p 4.
Row 19: K 4, p 2, k 4.

Row 20: P 4, sl 2 k sts to dpn, hold in front of work, p 1, k 2 sts from dpn, p 3.
Row 21: K 5, p 2, k 3.
Row 22: P 5, sl same as above, p 2.
Row 23: K 6, p 2, k 2.
Row 24: P 6, same as above, p 1.
Row 25: K 7, p 2, k 1, continue from Row 2, four more times.
Cast off.
With crochet hook size 0 sc in each st on edge across, break off and pull in strand with hook.

Finishing: Block each piece and steam on wrong side. Edges must be flat. To join panels and strips, place wrong sides together with strip facing you. Use yarn to match strip. Pin to ease in and sc together. Always work with strip facing you. Continue until all panels are joined. Measure for lining. With underside of sleeve facing you, sc to sleeve panel. Measure for lining. Sc other side. Finish second sleeve. Sew shoulder seams. With shoulder panel facing you, sc to upper coat section. Sc sleeve to upper coat. Shoulder panel should be facing you and there will be about 3½″ for side seam on shoulder panel. Upper section of coat, facing you, is attached to lower section with sc and contrasting color.

NECK RIBBING:

With Cherry and size 8 needles, pick up 24 sts on each side of neck and 38 sts from back holder—86 sts. Work in k 2, p 2 ribbing for 5 rows. Att Burgundy and work across k 2 Cherry, p 2 Burgundy. Work 3 more rows of 2-color ribbing. Det Cherry and work 4 rows ribbing in Burgundy. Cast off.
Pin long Burgundy strips to front of coat. They should match the top of neck ribbing. With strips facing, sc in place. Sew Blue collar to top of ribbing.
At lower edge, beg on wrong side, work 2 rows sc across entire edge.
Use lining pieces to cut polyester batting. Padding should be same size as coat, lining should have 1″ seam allowance. Place fill over coat sections and pin in place. Pin lining in place over fill turning in seam allowance. Hand-stitch in place. Hand-quilt between blocks through all layers of knitting, batting, and lining.
If desired, front bands may be backed with ribbon. Sew on snaps.

Mohair Dress

Sizes and Measurements:

The length of the dress is 47″ from shoulder to lower edge. Make dress longer by repeating stripes before waist ribbing, starting with Lilac, work until desired length.

Width of blouse = 23″.

waist = 16″.

skirt = 28″.

(These are approximate measurements.)

Materials:

Lightweight mohair, 2 skeins each of Corn Mist and Sea Mist. Mohair, 3 skeins of Lilac, 1 skein each of Cranberry and Lime.

Medium-weight bouclé, 3 skeins of Hyacinth Glo.

Sport-weight, 3 skeins of Teal.

Hooks:

Aluminum crochet sizes 0 and G, or sizes to obtain gauge.

Needles:

Sizes 8 and 10, or sizes to obtain gauge.

Gauge:

On size 10 needles, approx 3 sts = 1″ in pattern areas; 4 sts = 1″ in st st.

Pattern:

Row 1: * P 4, m 1 dbl (wool twice around needle). Rep from * across row, end, p 4.

Row 2: * K 2 tog twice, k into front and back of made st. Rep from * across row, end k 2 tog, twice.

Row 3: * P 1, m 1 dbl. Rep from * across row, end p 1.

Row 4: K 1, * k into front and back of made st, k 2 tog twice. Rep from * across row, end k 1.

Note 1: The right side of the dress is the purl side.

Note 2: Please note that part of the skirt does not have interlacing stripes as the lower area, so remember, if an area is purl on the front, you will purl on the back so that there is a clean strip. If you end in a knit stripe on the front and your next pattern is purled, purl across the back in your new color, then continue pattern.

BACK AND FRONT ARE THE SAME:

Begin: With size 10 needles and Teal homespun, cast on 88 sts. Work in patterns for 9 rows, ending on wrong side. Knit 10th row. Attach Hyacinth. On front, purl across. Work 9 rows, ending on purl side. Follow Note 2. Attach Lilac. On back knit across. On front start pattern, work 9 rows. Knit last row. Attach Hyacinth. On front side purl. Knit on back for 4 rows. Rep these rows with Cranberry, Teal, Sea Mist, Lime, and Lilac.

Rep stripes in same order, purling on front side in sequence of rows of three, rows of two, then 1 row of each color. Attach Teal. On front side, knit across.
On back, knit across.
On front, start pattern and work for 10 rows.
Attach Hyacinth. Purl on front, k on back, for 9 rows.
Attach Lilac. Knit on front, then back. On Row 3 start pattern work for 12 rows, ending knit on back. For Waist change to size 8 needles. Right side, p 1, k 2, p 2 across, ending k 2, p 1. Attach Hyacinth. Work 4 more rows.
Attach Cranberry. Work 1 row ribbing. Attach Teal. Work 5 rows ribbing. Attach Lilac. Work 1 row ribbing.

Attach Hyacinth. Work 6 rows ribbing.
Attach Cranberry. Work 1 row ribbing.

TWISTED RIBBING:

Row 1: On front side attach Teal. P 1, * insert needle from front through second k st on needle, pull yarn through to front, then k into the back of first st. Slip these off needle, p 2. Rep from * across, end p 1.
Row 2: K 1, * p 2, k 2. Rep from * across, end k 1. Work 10 rows in twisted ribbing.
Row 11, front: P 1, twist 2 k sts, * p 1, attach Corn Mist between these 2 purl sts and k 1 st, p 1, k twist, p 2, k twist. Rep from * across, end p 1.
Row 12, back: K 1, p 2, * k 1, p 1 Corn Mist, k 1, p 2, k 2, p 2. Rep from * across, end, k 1.
Row 13, front: P 1, * twist 2 k sts, k 3 Corn Mist, k 2, p 2, k 2. Rep

from * across, end p 1. Continue through row 17, inc 2 Corn Mist sts every other row and dec ribs.

Row 18: K 1 * p 7 Corn Mist, k 2 tog Teal. Rep from * across, end k 1.

Row 19, front: K across in Corn Mist.

Row 20: Purl across.

Row 21: Change to size 10 needles. Purl across.

Row 22: Knit.

Row 23: Purl.

Row 24, back: K 2 * p 5, k 3, rep from *, end k 2.

Row 25: P 2, * k 5, p 3, rep from *, end p 2.

Rows 26 through 28: Work 3 more rows of pattern (5 altogether).

Row 29: Purl.

Row 30: Knit.

Row 31: Purl.

Row 32: K 3, * p 3, k 5, rep from *, end k 3.

Row 33, front: P 3, * k 3, p 5, rep from *, end p 3. Work 3 more rows in pattern.

Next 3 rows are purled on front.

Work in patterns until there are 5 rows of purl stripe between check pattern. The last 3 rows of purl are neck edge. In pattern, work 29 sts, place 31 sts on holder, work 29 sts in pattern.

SHOULDER:

Row 1: On front, work across.

Row 2: Dec 1 st each side near neck edge as you continue in pattern.

Row 3: Work across.

Row 4: Dec each side at neck edge.

Row 5: Work across.

Row 6: Purl across, dec 1 st each side at neck edge.

Row 7: Knit.

Row 8: Purl. Dec 1 st each side at neck edge.

Row 9: Work pattern across.

Row 10: Work in pattern. Dec 1 st each side at neck edge.

Row 11: Work across in pattern, (24 sts left on each side).

Row 12: Work across in pattern.

Row 13: Work across in pattern.

Row 14: Purl across, dec 1 st each side at neck edge—23 sts left on shoulder.

Row 15, back: Change to size 8 needles and with Cranberry, p on 23 sts of shoulder, pick up 11 sts on neck in purl, then 31 sts on holder. Pick up 10 sts on neck, purl 24 on other side of shoulder.

Row 1, front: Purl 25 sts, * twist 2 sts, knit-wise, p 2 across 50 sts, purl 25 sts.

Row 2, back: K 25 sts, p 2, k 2 across 50 sts, k 25 sts.

Row 3, front: Work same as Row 1.

Row 4, back: Same as Row 2.

Attach Hyacinth. Work in same pattern for 3 rows. Purl across 25 sts, cast off 50 sts, work 25 sts on other shoulder, break off.

Attach Lilac on shoulder (working 1 side at a time). Work in purl on front side for 4 rows.

Attach Teal, work 4 rows.

Attach Sea Mist, work 4 rows.

Attach Lime, work 3 rows. Bind off on 4th row. Repeat for other side.

Finishing: Block lightly. Join shoulder seams in Lime thread. Then with Hyacinth and crochet hook O, join at corner on Hyacinth stripe on shoulder and sc, spacing evenly 20 sts to other hyacinth stripe. Continue on back, spacing 15 sc over the 20 previously made. Break off. Repeat on other shoulder. Sew side seams of dress with yarn to match stripes. Leave 12″ open from center seam of shoulder for deep armhole.

White Iris Embroidery (OPTIONAL):

Materials:

D.M.C. embroidery floss, 2 skeins each of variegated Lime Green and White, 1 each of Salmon Pink, Kelly Green, and Dark Yellow.

Embroidery sharp needle.
9″ or 10″ Plastic embroidery hoop (Note: This type of hoop has a screw that controls the tension of the fabric, even though heavy in weight).

One piece of sheer, white, lightweight blouse interfacing 10″ sq.

All of the yarn is 6-ply split into 3-ply pieces for work.
Position your hoop about 7″ from right side and 5½″ from hem. Dress has been blocked and the knit is flat, so do not pull excessively. Start a chain in Lime Green cotton a little over ¼″

from the edge of the hoop. Work for 2 rows in a circle. Take interfacing and baste it to the back of the knit inside hoop. For those who can follow a pattern free-hand, begin stitches as shown on pattern and refer to picture. If this is too difficult, you can trace the Iris on your interfacing in soft pencil, or water-fast, light-colored pen. Baste on top of work. Do your work on top. Press so that it is flat. Then with fine shears, cut excess facing to edge. Last but not least, chain on edge or purchase pre-made embroidery of your choice and lightly baste on from the back.

Striped Gray Pullover

This sweater is based on Irish countryside textures.

Materials:

1 ¼ lbs. sport- or worsted-weight wool. Colors and yarns are optional. I used the following:
> Pale Gray
> Beige Gray
> Olive Mist mohair
> Slate Black
> Black and Gray tweed

Hook:

Size 0 steel crochet, or size to obtain gauge.

Needles:

Sizes 9 and 8; size 8 dp needle.

Gauge:

On size 9 needles in st st, approx 4 sts = 1″, 5 rows = 1″.

Sizes and Measurements:

Directions given are for Small to Medium sizes.
For Large sizes, the whole sweater is worked on size 9 needles.
For Small to Medium sizes, the ribbing and body are worked on size 8 needles only. The sleeve ribbing and first knit and purl strip are worked on size 8 needles. Use size 9 for the rest of the sleeve.
The length from center back neck to ribbing is 25″.
The width of first Olive Mist stripe is approx 18″.
Sleeve length approx 13″.
Sleeve width at top, 18″.
Front inset, 9 to 9½″ long.

FRONT:

With size 8 needles cast on 74 sts in Beige Gray, work ribbing in k 2 p 2.

Note: in order to avoid a loose, sloppy look on the ribbing, I knitted the sts (on the front side only) by twisting each one for 4½″, ending with work to front.

Attach Black and Gray tweed, knit across. Purl across. On front start pattern. Oblique openwork has a multiple of 2.

Row 1: K 1, * wool around needle (wrn) to make 1, k 2 tog, rep from * across, k 1.

Row 2: Purl.

Row 3: K 2, * m 1, k 2 tog. Rep from *.

Row 4: Purl. Do this pattern for 10 rows. Then on front, knit across—(13 rows).

Row 14: Inc row. Attach Olive Mist. (Note: It is less confusing to increase on simple row, and pattern of previous row flairs out naturally.) Purl across.

Next rows: Work in garter stitch (purl on front and back of stripe) for 10 rows. Inc each side three times on third, fifth, and seventh rows, on last row, have 1 st extra inc—81 sts.

(Note: The extra st is for balancing the cable pattern.)

Front: Attach Beige Gray and knit across.

Back: K 1, * p 4, k 1, rep from * across.

Front: Start of 4 st cable. P 1, * sl next 2 sts to dpn and hold in back, (or in front); k 2, k 2 from dpn, p 1. Rep from * across.

Back: K 1, * p 4, k 1. Rep from * across.

Front: P 1, * k 4, p 1. Rep from * across.

Back: K 1, * p 4, k 1. Rep from * across.

Front: Rep cable row.

Back: K 1, * p 4, k 1. Rep from * across.

Front: Knit straight across.

  Attach Slate Black.

Back: Purl.

Front: K 2, p 2 for 40 sts, ending p 2, k 2 p 2, k 2 for 40 sts.

Note: On Slate Black last row, work in pattern for 25 sts, cast off 31 sts, work rem 25 sts in pattern.

Attach Olive Mist mohair. Back: Purl across. Do each 25 sts in garter st for 11 rows. End on wrong side.

Attach Black and Gray tweed. Front: Knit across each set of 25 sts, increasing 1 st on outside edge, 26 sts each side. Back: Purl.

Note: Pattern is worked in multiple of 2s.

Follow pattern for row above ribbing.

Do this pattern for 12 rows. Last row, front: Knit across both sides, 13 rows.

Attach Beige Gray. Back: Purl across both sides.

Front: Start pattern, Trinity stitch has a multiple of 4.

Row 1: Purl across.

Row 2, back: K 1, * (k 1, p 1, k 1) into the 1st stitch, p 3 tog. Rep from * across, k 1. K 1 at each edge, takes care of extra two sts of pattern.

Row 3, front: Purl.

Row 4, back: K 1, * p 3 tog (k 1, p 1, k 1) into the next st, rep from * across, k 1.

Row 5: Purl, for front. From Row 2, rep pattern four more times, ending on back. Knit across both sides.

Attach Pale Gray. Work in pattern, Vandyke stitch.

FRONT:

Row 1: * K 5, wrn to m 1, k 2 tog, k 1 Rep from * across, k 2.
Back: Purl next row and all alt rows.

Row 3: * K 3, k 2 tog, m 1, k 1, m 1, k 2 tog, rep from * across, k 2.

Row 5: K 1, * k 1, k 2 tog tbl, m 1, k 3, m 1, k 2 tog. Rep. from * across, k 1.

Row 7: * M 1, k 2 tog tbl, put st back on left-hand needle and pass next st on left-hand needle over it, put st back on right-hand needle, m 1, k 5. Rep from * across, k 2.

Row 9: * K 1, k into front and back of next st, k 6. Rep from * across, k 1.

Row 11: * K 2 tog, k 4, m 1, K 2 tog, k 1. Rep from * across, k 2.
Rep from Row 3 to Row 7.

Next Row: Rep Row 5. Then Row 3, and Row 1.

SHOULDERS:

Next Row: Pale Gray. Back: Cast off 4 sts, p across. K 1 row. Cast off 4 sts at beg of next p row. K 1 row. Cast off 4 sts the next p row. K 1 row. Cast off 14 sts. Work other side to correspond. End with cast-off sts on k side.

BACK:

Work even up to Beige Gray, Trinity st. Omit casting off for front inset. Attach Pale Gray and work across in pattern. There will be 81 sts so your pattern will start out with 1 inc st at each side, 83 sts, on first row. Work row 1 of Vandyke stitch and continue pattern across the same as front. You will have 9 triangles with 2 halves at the ends and 10 full diamonds. Cast off for shoulders the same as for front. Cast off rem sts for back neck.

SLEEVES:

In Pale Gray with size 8 needles, cast on 46 sts. Work in k 2, p 2 for 6 rows. On front side inc 1 st between purl 2s in knit across—57 sts. P across 1 row. Inc 1 st each side every 3 rows three times—63 sts. Continue in st st from first inc row after 6 rows of ribbing for 13 rows. On 14th row, change to purl on front of work. Inc 3 sts each side on third row—69 sts. From 14th row, work purl on front for 13 rows. Change to size 9 needles, and st st. Knit on front side for 13 rows. For the next 13 rows, purl on front. Attach Gray Black tweed yarn, purl across. Front side: Start pattern of first stripe of sweater in oblique openwork.

Finishing: Block sweater with a damp cloth and iron on wrong side. Don't press down areas of mohair or ribbing. When joining sweater join in yarn the same color as stripes. At the shoulder edge (after seams are sewn) place open sleeve to edge. If the sleeve should be a little smaller than the measure from pattern of front to back ease together and join from inside. See Front panel is set in from wrong side.

Front Panel: With Pale Gray yarn and size 8 needles, cast on 30 sts. P 1 row.

Row 1, Pattern Front: *Row 1 of Fern pattern*—* K 1, sl 1, k 2 tog, psso, k 9, wrn to m 1, k 1, m 1, p 2, m 1, k 1, m 1, k 9, sl 1, k 2 tog, psso, k 1.

Row 2, and all even rows: P 14, k 2, p 14.

Row 3: * K 1, sl 1, k 2 tog, psso, k 8 (m 1, k 1) twice, p 2 (k 1, m 1) twice, k 8, sl 1, k 2 tog, psso, k 1.

Row 5: K 1, sl 1, k 2 tog, psso, k 7, m 1, k 1, m 1, k 2, p 2, k 2, m 1, k 1, m 1, k 7, sl 1, k 2 tog, psso, k 1.

Row 7: K 1, sl 1, k 2 tog, psso, k 6, m 1, k 1, m 1, k 3, p 2, k 3, m 1, k 1, m 1, k 6, sl 1, k 2 tog, psso, k 1.

Row 9: K 1, sl 1, k 2 tog, psso, k 5, m 1, k 1, m 1, k 4, p 2, k 4, m 1, k 1, m 1, k 5, sl 1, k 2 tog, psso, k 1.

There are now 5 vertical rows of holes for fern patterns.

Row 10: Rep Row 2.

For the 2nd section of the leaf pattern, rep Rows 1 through 10, then add this row:

Row 11: K 1, sl 1, k 2 tog, psso, k 4, m 1, k 1, m 1, k 5, p 2, k 5, m 1, k 1, m 1, k 4, sl 1, k 2 tog, psso, k 1.

Row 12: Rep Row 2.

3rd Section: Work pattern up to Row 6.

Row 7: K 1, sl 1, k 2 tog, psso, k 6, m 1, k 1, m 1, k 2, m 1, k 1, m 1, p 2, m 1, k 1, m 1, k 2, m 1, k 1, m 1, k 6, sl 1, k 2 tog, psso, k 1.

Row 8: P 16, k 2, p 16.

Row 9: K 1, sl 1, k 2 tog, psso, k 5, m 1, k 1, m 1, k 4, m 1, k 1, m 1, k 1, p 2, k 1, m 1, k 1, m 1, k 4, m 1, k 1, m 1, k 5, sl 1, k 2 tog, psso, k 1.

Row 10: P 18, k 2, p 18.

Row 11: K 1, sl 1, k 2 tog, psso, k 4, m 1, k 1, m 1, k 6, m 1, k 1, m 1, k 2, p 2, k 2, m 1, k 1, m 1, k 6, m 1, k 1, m 1, k 4, sl 1, k 2 tog, psso, k 1.

Row 12: P 20, k 2, p 20.

Row 13: K 1, sl 1, k 2 tog, psso, k 12, m 1, k 4, p 2, k 4, m 1, k 12, sl 1, k 2 tog, psso, k 1.

Row 14: P 19, k 2, p 19.

Row 15: K 1, sl 1, k 2 tog, psso, k 13, k 2 tog, p 2, k 2 tog, k 13, sl 1, k 2 tog, psso, k 1.

Row 16: P 16, k 2, p 16.

Row 17: K 1, sl 1, k 2 tog, psso, k 10, k 2 tog, p 2, k 2 tog, k 10, sl 1, k 2 tog, psso, k 1.

Row 18: P 13, k 2, p 13.

Row 19: Cast off.

Row 19: Bind off. When this piece is finished it takes on a curve at the bottom which cannot be blocked out. Block the piece first. On bottom with your crochet hook beg sc 4 sts from edge of m 1 for Fern. There will be 13 sts, which should work to 4 sts from other edge. Break off. Attach yarns again and beg sc, at third st from edge. Sc into 13 sts, then 1 sc past—15 sts. Break off.

With your crochet hook, and mohair sc in each cast off st around neck . Skip 1 st, two times each corner of neck. Block neck and front panels after finishing.

Attach yarn at edge of work at the bottom and work across each in sc to other edge. Break off.

Linda Mendelson

Linda Mendelson, who has been knitting since she was five years old, was taught by an ambidextrous mother who never has to turn her work to start a new row of knitting. This is the way a knitting machine knits and it may have been a premonition of what was in Linda's future—that she would one day become one of the country's foremost machine knitters. Her extraordinary machine-knit garments are shown exclusively in New York at that city's leading creative crafts gallery, Julie: Artisans' Gallery.

A section of Elyse Sommer's A New Look at Knitting featured Linda at her knitting machine. Her work also appears in Knitting and Clothing Decoration. Her own book, Creative Machine Knitting which she co-authored with Mark Dittrick, is scheduled for publication in the spring of 1979. Linda recently began designing machine knits for Ladies' Home Journal Needle & Craft, the first major crafts magazine to carry machine-knit garment instructions as a regular feature.

"*I am a meticulous planner. Before I start to knit a garment I plan it down to the last stitch. A lot of the things I design I don't actually knit myself; I have someone knit them for me by following my very detailed instructions. If there's anything wrong with them, I hear about it very quickly from the person who's doing the knitting for me.*

"I do both hand knitting and machine knitting—fifty–fifty. If I hadn't taken up machine knitting I probably would never have started designing hand knits. Up until the time I bought my first knitting machine all my hand knitting was done either from pattern books or from magazines. When I started machine knitting I found that there were no patterns available—at least nothing that I found at all worth knitting—so I was forced to design my own. When I realized that I could design things for the machine, I went back and discovered that I could also design my own hand knits. Why, I wondered, hadn't I tried before?

"Machine knitting is growing like crazy, and more designs are becoming available. Some of the magazines that have traditionally had only hand-knitted things are beginning to include machine-knit garments, and I'm just now starting to design for them. Knitters who take up working on a machine shouldn't worry that they'll end up dropping their handwork. I haven't and I never will. I think it's like being an actress or actor who performs on the stage and also makes movies. You can do both, even though they're quite different."

Linda Mendelson

Lacy Armor Vest

Inspired by a suit of samurai armor, the scale-like stitch pattern and pagoda shoulders are framed by a traditional Shetland lace knitting pattern which is turned upside down after it is knitted.

Size:

One size fits all.

Materials:

Rug, colossal, or bulky-weight yarn, 20 oz.

Needles:

Size 10½, or size to obtain gauge.

Gauge:

One motif = 3½".

Pattern:

Row 1: Purl.
Row 2: K 1 * yo, k 3, sl 1, 2 tog, psso, k 3, yo, k 1 * Rep from * to *.
Row 3: Purl.
Row 4: P 1 * k 1, yo, k 2, sl 1, k 2 tog, psso, k 2, yo, k 1, p 1 *, Rep from * to *.
Row 5: K 1 * p 9, k 1 *, rep from * to *.
Row 6: P 1 * k 2, yo, k 1, sl 1, k 2 tog, psso, k 1, yo, k 2, p 1 *, rep from * to *.
Row 7: K 1, * p 9, k 1 *, rep from * to *.
Row 8: P 1, * k 3, yo, sl 1, k 2 tog, psso, yo, k 3. p 1 *, rep from * to *.
Row 9: Purl.
Row 10: P 1, * yo, k 3, sl 1, k 2 tog, psso, k 3, yo, p 1 *, rep from * to *.
Row 11: Purl.
Row 12: P 1, * k 1, yo, k 2, sl 1, k 2 tog, psso, k 2, yo, k 1, p 1 *, rep from * to *.
Row 13: P 1, * k 1, p 7, k 1, p 1 *, rep from * to *.
Row 14: P 1, * k 1, p 1, yo, k 1, sl 1, k 2 tog, psso, k 1, yo. p 1, k 1, p 1 *, rep from * to *.

Row 15: P 1, * k 1, p 1, k 1, p 3, k 1, p 1, k 1, p 1 *, rep from * to *.

Row 16: P 1, * k 1, p 1, k 1, yo, sl 1, k 2 tog, psso, yo, k 1, p 1, k 1, p 1 *, rep from * to *.

Row 17: P 1, * k 1, p 1, k 1, p 3, k 1, p 1, k 1, p 1 *, rep from * to *.

Row 18: P 1, * k 1, p 1, k 2 tog, yo, k 1, yo, sl 1, k 1, psso, p 1, k 1, p 1 *, Rep from * to *.

BACK:

Cast on 61 sts.
Work Rows 1 through 8 of the pattern six times.
Work Rows 9 through 18 of the pattern.
Repeat Rows 17 and 18 of the pattern until the piece measures 19″ from the bottom points.
Bind off.

FRONT:

Make 2.
Cast on 31 sts. Work as for back.

Finishing: Press each piece. Sew the shoulder seams together between the first and second points. Sew the side seams, leaving 9″ openings for the armholes.

Bias-knit
Geometric Vest

This vest is knit on the bias. After knitting, the pieces require a lot of pressing to achieve a rectangular shape; therefore, an elastic yarn such as wool should be used.

Size:

Directions are for Small, Medium, and Large.

Materials:

Rug, colossal, or bulky-weight, 10, 10, 12 oz. each of Rust and Turquoise; 6, 6, 8 oz. Black.

Size J aluminum crochet hook.

Needles:

Size 10 long, straight.

Gauge:

None is given since the pieces are knitted by measurement alone.

BACK:

With Rust cast on 3 sts.
P 1 row.
K 1 row, inc in the 1st st and in the 2nd st.
P 1 row.
K 1 row, inc in the 1st st and in the 2nd st from the end of the row.
Rep last 2 rows until piece measures 18″, 19″, 20″ *along the diagonal edge.* End with a k row.
With Black p 1 row.
With Turquoise k 1, sl 1, k 1, pass sl st over (psso), k to within 3 sts from end of row, k 2 tog, k 1.
P 1 row.
Rep last 2 rows until 3 sts remain. Bind off.

FRONT:

Make 2.
With Rust cast on 3 sts.
Work as for back until piece measures 9″, 9½″, 10″ *along the diagonal edge.* End with a k row.

143

With Black p 1 row.

With Turquoise k, inc in the 1st st, k to within 3 sts from end of row, k 2 tog, k 1.

P 1 row.

Rep last 2 rows until piece measures 18″, 19″, 20″ *along the longest diagonal edge.* End with a k row.

With Black p 1 row.

With Rust work as for back, dec on both ends of each k row until 3 sts remain. Bind off.

Finishing: Block each piece several times, pulling the pieces into the desired rectangular shape. Let the pieces rest between pressings until you are certain that they will retain the desired shape.

With Black work 1 row of sc around each piece. With purl sides facing each other, crochet shoulder seams, leaving a 10″ opening for the neck.

Crochet side seams leaving 8″, 8″, 9″ openings for the armholes. Press again. Weave in all ends.

Boat-Neck Sweater

Size:

Directions are for Small, Medium, and Large.

Materials:

Sport-weight yarn in 6 shades ranging from light to dark.
The darkest shade is the main color (MC).

2 oz. each of colors (A), (B), (C), (D), and (E).
Color (A) is the lightest shade; color (B) one shade darker,
color (C) one shade darker than color (B), etc.

20, 22, 24 oz. of the darkest shade, (MC).

Size I aluminum crochet hook.

Needles:

Size 4 long, straight, or size to obtain gauge.

Gauge:

5 sts = 1″.

BACK AND FRONT:

Make 2.
With color A cast on 90, 95, 100 sts.
In garter st work 4 rows each of colors A, B, C, D, and E. With
MC work in seed st until 14″, 14″, 15″ from the beginning or
desired length to armhole.
Bind off 10, 12, 15 sts at beg of each of next 2 rows.
Cont working in seed st until 8″ above armhole.
In garter st work 4 rows each of colors E, D, C, B, and A.
Bind off all sts.

SLEEVES:

Make 2.

With color A, cast on 100 sts.

In garter st work 4 rows each of colors A, B, C, D, and E. With MC, work in seed st until 17½″ from beg. In garter st, work 4 rows each of colors E, D, C, B, and A. Bind off 32 sts at beg of each of next 2 rows. Cont working in garter st until 2″, 2½″, 3″ above the bound-off stitches.

Bind off all sts.

Finishing: Steam pieces gently.

With MC work 1 row of sc around each piece.

Crochet shoulder seams together leaving a 10″ opening for the neck.

Crochet the sleeves to the armholes.

Crochet the underarm and side seams. Weave in all the loose ends.

Jacket with Big Sleeves

Size:

Directions are for Small, Medium, and Large.

Materials:

Rug or colossal-weight yarn, 2 ¼ lbs.

Cranberry (MC)	6 oz.
Off-White (A)	4 oz.
Pale Rose (B)	4 oz.
Medium Rose (C)	4 oz.
Deep Rose (D)	4 oz.
Pale Gold (E)	4 oz.
Medium Gold (F)	4 oz.
Deep Gold (G)	4 oz.
Orange (H)	4 oz.
Red (J)	4 oz.

11 Buttons.
¾" Grosgrain ribbon to match MC.
Size J aluminum crochet hook.

Needles:

Size 10½, 36" circular.

Gauge:

5 sts = 2".

STRIPES:

Rows	Color	Rows	Color
7	A	2	B
1	B	1	A
2	A	3	B
1	B	1	E
2	A	2	B
2	B	1	E
1	A	1	F

Rows	Color		Rows	Color
2	E		1	F
1	F		2	G
2	E		1	D
2	F		2	G
1	E		4	D
4	F		1	G
1	C		4	D
1	F		2	G
1	B		2	D
2	C		1	C
2	F		4	G
2	C		2	H
1	E		2	G
4	F		2	H
1	C		2	J
1	D		2	G
2	F		2	H
1	C		1	J

The remainder of the jacket is knitted in the main color, MC.

BODY:

Same for all sizes. With scrap of contrasting color yarn, cast on 80 sts. Work in st st following the stripes until piece measures 22½″ from the beg. End with a p row.

On next row k 40 sts and place the rem 40 sts on a heavy piece of scrap yarn which will function as a stitch holder. Continuing to follow stripes, k the 40 sts in st st until 8″ above dividing point. End with a k row. At beg of next row, cast on 40 sts. Work in st st until 22″ from the 40 cast-on sts. Thread a heavy piece of yarn through all the sts to act as a holder. Pick up first 40 sts, which are being held. Continuing to follow stripes, bind off 5 sts at center edge. Dec 1 st at center edge every other row five times. K rem 30 sts until 5″ above the beg of the neckline shaping. Inc 1 st at center edge every other row five times. Cast on 5 sts at center edge. K 3 rows. Bind off.

Note: Press the piece before knitting cuffs, waistband, or collar.

RIGHT CUFF:

Rip out the contrasting color yarn of the cast-on row and place sts on needle with the face of the stockinette towards you. K 1, then k 2 tog across row. P one row. K 4, k 2 tog sixteen times, k 4. Work these 24 sts in k 3 p 3 ribbing for 6″. Bind off loosely.

LEFT CUFF:

With the knit side facing you, place sts being held on yarn back on needles. K 2 tog across row. P 1 row. K 4, k 2 tog sixteen times, k 4. Work ribbing as for right cuff.

BACK WAISTBAND:

Using MC and with purl side facing you, pick up 42, 45, 48 sts across center of lower edge of back. Work these sts in k 3, p 3 ribbing for 6″. Bind off loosely.

RIGHT FRONT WAISTBAND:

Using MC and with purl side facing you, pick up 36, 39, 41 sts across bottom edge of right front, making sure that sts match waistband on back when the sweater is folded over. Work these sts in k 3, p 3 ribbing for 6″. Bind off loosely.

LEFT FRONT WAISTBAND:

Using MC and with purl side facing you, pick up 6, 6, 6, sts across bottom edge of left front. Work these sts in k 3, p 3, ribbing for 6″. Bind off loosely.

COLLAR:

Pick up 46 sts evenly spaced around neckline. Work in garter st for 5½″. K 1 row each of colors H, G, MC, J, and H. Cont knitting with MC in garter st until collar measures 13″. Bind off loosely.

Finishing: Press the collar. With purl sides inside, sew underarm and side seams. (The purl side is the right side.) Work 1 row sc along front openings and collar edge. Sew grosgrain ribbon inside both front edges. Sew buttons evenly spaced along left front edge. Crochet buttonholes by crocheting a loop of 2 or 3 chains to correspond to each button. The size of the loop will depend on the size of the buttons. Weave in all ends.

Rainbow Coat

Size:

One size fits all.

Materials:

Worsted-weight yarn.

Purple (A)	4 oz.
Blue Violet (B)	4 oz.
Blue (C)	4 oz.
Blue Green (D)	4 oz.
Green (E)	4 oz.
Yellow Green (F)	4 oz.
Yellow (G)	4 oz.
Yellow-Orange (H)	4 oz.
Orange (J)	4 oz.
Red Orange (K)	4 oz.
Red (L)	4 oz.
Magenta (M)	4 oz.

Rug or colossal-weight yarn.

Gray	3 lbs. (48 oz.)

Size J aluminum crochet hook.

Needles:

Size 10½ long, straight, or size to obtain gauge.

Gauge:

Stockinette st: 5 sts = 2″, 15 rows = 4″.
Seed st: 11 sts = 4″.

Note: As 4 strands of worsted will be used, each color must be wound into 4 balls before starting to knit. To avoid tangled balls of yarn while knitting, place the 4 balls with which you are working in a shoebox and thread the ends through 4 holes punched in the top of the shoebox.

BACK SLEEVES AND YOKE:

With 4 strands of color A, cast on 33 sts (AAAA = 4 strands of color A).

K 9 rows in st st.

Break off 1 strand of color A and replace it with 1 strand of color B (AAAB = 3 strands color A, one strand color B).

K 9 rows in st st.

Break off 1 strand of color A and replace it with 1 strand of color B. (AABB = two strands color A, two strands color B).

K 9 rows st st.

Using the following chart k 9 rows in st st in each color combination:

ABBB	DDDE
BBBB	DDEE
BBBC	DEEE
BBCC	EEEE
BCCC	EEEF
CCCC	EEFF
CCCD	EFFF
CCDD	EFFF
CDDD	FFFF
DDDD	

After knitting 9 rows with FFFF bind off all the sts.

RIGHT SLEEVE AND YOKE:

With 4 strands of color G (GGGG), cast on 33 sts.

K as for back working 9 rows of each of the following color combinations.

GGGG	HHJJ
GGGH	HJJJ
GGHH	JJJJ
GHHH	JJJK
HHHH	JJKK
HHHJ	

After knitting 9 rows with JJKK bind off all the sts.

LEFT SLEEVE AND YOKE:

With colors JJKK cast on 33 sts.

K as for back working 9 rows of each of the following color combinations:

```
JJKK          LLLL
JKKK          LLLM
KKKK          LLMM
KKKL          LMMM
KKLL          MMMM
KLLL
```

After knitting 9 rows with MMMM bind off all the sts.

BACK BODY:

    With Gray rug-weight yarn, cast on 60 sts.
    Work in seed st for 22″.
    Bind off all the sts.

FRONT BODY:

    Make 2.
    With Gray rug-weight yarn, cast on 32 sts.
    Work in seed st for 22″.
    Bind off all the sts.

    Finishing: Press all the pieces.
    Using Gray yarn work 1 row of sc around each piece.
    With the purl sides outward (the purl side is used as the right side) crochet shoulder and sleeve seams together, leaving a 10″ opening for the neck.
    Crochet body pieces to the yokes.
    Crochet underarm and side seams leaving 9″ slits on the sides of the body. Weave in all the ends.

Andrée Rubin

Andrée Rubin ranks high on the list of top designers who work for the country's leading yarn companies. Her garments and designs appear in instructional brochures published by these companies, in their advertisements, or in the pages of women's magazines and needlecraft publications. While she doesn't work exclusively for any one yarn company, the combined names of Andrée Rubin and William Unger are as familiar to knitters as Don Meredith and Lipton are to tea drinkers. Other companies lucky enough to have Andrée Rubin design for them include Spinnerin, Monsanto, and Tahki.

"*I* *often find myself knitting with synthetics because one of the companies I do a lot of work for, William Unger, manufactures an extensive line of very high quality synthetic yarns. There's nothing worse to knit with than a cheap synthetic, but a really good one can produce some very beautiful garments. Lurex is a good example of a synthetic yarn I can work with: It's a yarn with more shine than metallic yarn, but it's not a metallic shininess. And Lurex is the only synthetic I'll block with an iron. Using an iron on Lurex gives it more shine and adds to its shimmery quality. I block it with water and steam and it reacts beautifully. Other synthetics hate heat, and blocking them with an iron and steam will ruin them.*

"Another thing that can ruin a knitted garment, no matter what type of yarn is used, is poor assembly. Crocheting is perfectly acceptable for joining sections of knitting, but I prefer sewing or weaving. If a sleeve is the set-in type, I'll sew it. If there's extra fullness in the sleeve, I always keep the excess material away from the shoulder seam: I gather it to the lower part of the sleeve to avoid bunching or a pushed-out look at the shoulder. When I weave sections together, I put them face to face and then work into the fronts of the two pieces. I catch the second half of each end stitch and weave with a needle and thread through that part of the stitch. Then I catch the second half of the corresponding end stitch in the other piece and weave through it. I just keep working back and forth that way until both sides are joined. If this is done really well it results in an almost invisible seam."

Andrée Rubin

Gold Donegal Tweed
Aran Isle Hooded Jacket

Sizes:

Directions are for bust sizes 30" to 32". Changes for sizes 34" to 36" and 38" are in parentheses.

Measurements:

Finished width around underarm 35" (38", 40½").

Materials:

Knitting worsted-weight Donegal Tweed homespun, 4-oz. skeins, 9 (10, 11) Gold.

Size J aluminum crochet hook.

Heavy duty separating zipper.

Needles:

Sizes 5 and 11, or size to obtain gauge; 1 cable or double-pointed (dp).

Gauge:

On size 11 needles with 2 strands of yarn held tog, in st st and Moss st, 3 sts = 1", 4½ rows = 1". In Aran patts, 4 sts = 1", 4½ rows = 1".

Abbreviations:

Twist Knit (called K 1 b): Working through back of st, k 1, twisting st.
Twist Purl (called P 1 b): Working through back of st, p 1, twisting st.
Left Twist (called LT): Sl next 2 sts on a dp needle, hold in front of work, p 1, k 2 off dp needle.
Right Twist (called RT): Sl next st on a dp needle, hold in back of work, k 2, p 1 off dp needle.
4 St Cable (called 4 C): Sl next 2 sts on a dp needle, hold in front of work, k 2, k 2 off dp needle.

PATT 1:

(Moss st worked over an uneven number of sts):
Rows 1 and 4: K 1, * p 1, k 1, rep from * to end.
Rows 2 and 3: P 1, * k 1, p 1, rep from * to end. Rep these 4 rows
for Patt 1.

PATT 2:

(Twist Rib worked over 1 st):
Row 1 (right side): K 1 b.
Row 2: P 1 b. Rep these 2 rows for Patt 2.

PATT 3:

(Double Zigzag worked over 16 (18, 18) sts):
Row 1 (right side): P O (1, 1), k 2, p 3, k 2, p 2, k 2, p 3, k 2, P O (1,
1).
Row 2 and all even rows through 16: On wrong side, k the knit
sts and p the purl sts.
Row 3: P O (1, 1), LT, p 2, LT, RT, p 2, RT, P O (1, 1).
Row 5: P 1 (2, 2) LT, p 2, 4 C, p 2, RT, p 1 (2, 2).
Row 7: P 2 (3, 3), LT, RT, LT, RT, p 2 (3, 3).
Row 9: P 3 (4, 4), 4 C, p 2, 4 C, p 3 (4, 4).
Row 11: P 2 (3, 3), RT, LT, RT, LT, p 2 (3, 3).
Row 13: P 1 (2, 2), RT, p 2, 4 C, p 2, LT, p 1 (2, 2).
Row 15: P O (1, 1), RT p 2, RT, LT, p 2, LT, P O (1, 1). Rep Rows 3
through 16 for Patt 3.

PATT 4:

(Diamond and Cable worked over 10 (10, 12) sts:
Row 1 (right side): P 3 (3, 4), k 4, p 3 (3–4).
Row 2 and all even rows through 16: On wrong side, k the knit
sts and p the purl sts.
Row 3: P 2 (2, 3), RT, LT, p 2 (2, 3).
Row 5: P 1 (1, 2), RT, p 2, LT, p 1 (1, 2).
Row 7: P 1 (1, 2), LT, p 2, RT, p 1 (1, 2).
Row 9: P 2 (2–3), LT, RT, p 2 (2, 3).
Rows 11 and 15: P 3 (3, 4), 4 C, p 3 (3, 4).
Row 13: Rep Row 1. Rep Rows 3 through 16 for Patt 4.

Note: Ribbed bands are worked using a single strand of yarn.
All other parts of jacket are worked with 2 strands of yarn held
tog.

BACK:

With size 5 needles and 1 strand, cast on 69, (75, 79) sts. Work in k 1, p 1, ribbing to 3″, inc 1 st each end of last row—71 (77, 81) sts. Join a 2nd strand of yarn. Change to size 11 needles and patts.

Row 1: Work Row 1 of Patt 1 over 5 sts, Row 1 of Patt 2 over 1 st, Row 1 of Patt 3 over 16 (18, 18) sts, Row 1 of Patt 2 over 1 st, Row 1 of Patt 4 over 10 (10, 12) sts, Row 1 of Patt 2 over 1 st. p 3 (5, 5), (center panel worked in reverse st st throughout), Row 1 of Patt 2 over 1 st, Row 1 of Patt 4 over 10 (10, 12) sts, Row 1 of Patt 2 over 1 st, Row 1 of Patt 3 over 16 (18, 18) sts, Row 1 of Patt 2 over 1 st, Row 1 of Patt 1 over 5 sts.

Row 2: Work Row 2 of Patt 1 over 5 sts, Row 2 of Patt 2 over 1 st, Row 2 of Patt 3 over 16 (18, 18) sts, Row 2 of Patt 2 over 1 st, Row 2 of Patt 4 over 10 (10, 12) sts, Row 2 of Patt 2 over 1 st, k 3 (5, 5), Row 2 of Patt 2 over 1 st, Row 2 of Patt 4 over 10 (10, 12) sts, Row 2 of Patt 2 over 1 st, Row 2 of Patt 3 over 16 (18, 18) sts, Row 2 of Patt 2 over 1 st, Row 2 of Patt 1 over 5 sts. Keeping to patts as established, work to 15″ from beg. End ready for a right side row.

Shape Armholes: Keeping to patts, bind off 4 sts at beg of next 2 rows—63 (69, 73) sts. Work even until armholes measure 8 (8½″, 9″). End ready for a right side row.

Shape Shoulders: Bind off 18 (20, 20) sts, work 27 (29, 33) sts, sl to a holder for hood, bind off rem 18 (20, 20) sts.

LEFT FRONT:

With size 5 needles and 1 strand, cast on 33 (35, 37) sts. Work in k 1, p 1 ribbing to 3″, inc 2 (3, 3) sts evenly across last row. 35 (38, 40) sts. Join a 2nd strand of yarn. Change to size 11 needles and patts.

Row 1: Work Row 1 of Patt 1 over 5 sts, Row 1 of Patt 2 over 1 st, Row 1 of Patt 3 over 16 (18, 18) sts, Row 1 of Patt 2 over 1 st, Row 1 of Patt 4 over 10 (10, 12) sts, Row 1 of Patt 2 over 1 st, p 1 (2, 2). (Front edge sts worked in reverse st st throughout).

Row 2: K 1 (2, 2), work Row 2 of Patt 2 over 1 st, Row 2 of Patt 4 over 10 (10, 12) sts, Row 2 of Patt 2 over 1 st, Row 2 of Patt 3 over 16 (18, 18) sts, Row 2 of Patt 2 over 1 st, Row 2 of Patt 1 over 5 sts. Keeping to patts as established, work to same length as back to underarm, ending at side edge.

Shape Armhole: Keeping to patts, bind off 4 sts at beg of next row. 31 (34, 36) sts. Work even until armhole measures same as back to shoulders, ending at side edge.

Shape Shoulder: Bind off 18 (20, 20) sts, sl rem 13 (14, 16) sts to a holder for hood.

RIGHT FRONT:

Work same as left front to Row 1 of patts.

Row 1: P 1 (2, 2), (front edge sts), work Row 1 of Patt 2 over 1 st, Row 1 of Patt 4 over 10 (10, 12) sts, Row 1 of Patt 2 over 1 st, Row 1 of Patt 3 over 16 (18, 18) sts, Row 1 of Patt 2 over 1 st, Row 1 of Patt 1 over 5 sts. Keeping to patts as established, work same as left front, reversing shaping. Sew shoulder seams.

HOOD:

From right side sl 13 (14, 16) sts from right front holder to a size 11 needle. K 27 (29, 33) sts off back holder, pick up 2 (1, 0) sts at shoulder seam, keeping to patt work 13 (14–16) sts off left front holder—57 (59, 65).

Row 1, wrong side: Keeping to patt, work 13 (14—16) sts. P, dec 0 (0, 2) sts evenly across next 31 (31, 33) sts—31 sts on all sizes. Keeping to patt work 13 (14, 16) sts.

Row 2: Keeping to patt work 13 (14, 16) sts, work Row 1 of Patt 1 over next 31 sts, keeping to patt work 13 (14, 16) sts. 57 (59, 63) sts. Continue in patts as established, keeping center 31 sts in Patt 1, until hood measures 14″ or desired length to top. Bind off all sts.

SLEEVES:

From right side working along straight edge of armhole, with size 11 needles and 2 strands of yarn pick up 54 (56, 60) sts. K one row. Beg patts.

Row 1: Work Row 1 of Patt 1 over 7 sts, Row 1 of Patt 2 over 1 st, Row 1 of Patt 4 over 10 (10, 12) sts, Row 1 of Patt 2 over 1 st, Row 1 of Patt 3 over 16 (18, 18) sts, Row 1 of Patt 2 over 1 st, Row 1 of Patt 4 over 10 (10, 12) sts, Row 1 of Patt 2 over 1 st, Row 1 of Patt 1 over 7 sts. Keeping to patts as established work 2″. Dec 1 st each end of next row, then every 2½″ (2½″, 2″) 5 (5, 6) times more—42 (44, 46) sts. Work even until sleeve measures 17″or 3″ less than desired length, end ready for a right side row. Break off one strand of yarn. Change to size 5 needles. K 1 row, dec 3 sts evenly across—39 (41, 43) sts. Work in p 1, k 1 ribbing for 3″. Bind off loosely in ribbing.

Finishing: Sew side and sleeve seams. Sew top of hood tog. From right side with crochet hook size J and 2 strands of yarn, beg at lower right front corner, work 1 row sc up right front, around hood and down left front to corner. Fasten off. Steam block. Sew zipper to front opening.

Gray Shetland
Cable Sweater
with Saddle Shoulders

Sizes:

Directions are for bust sizes 30″ to 32″. Changes for sizes 34″ to 36″ and 38″ are in parentheses.

Measurements:

Finished width around underarm 33¼″ (36″, 38¾″).

Materials:

Medium-weight 100 percent Shetland-type yarn, 1⅚₀-oz. balls, 8 (9, 10) Gray.

Needles:

Sizes 4 and 6, or sizes to obtain gauge; 1 cable or double-pointed (dp).

Gauge:

In st st, 6 sts = 1″, 7 rows = 1″.
In Cable Patt, 6 sts = 1″, 7 rows = 1″.

Abbreviations:

6 St Cable (C 6): Sl next 3 sts to a dp needle, hold in back of work, k 3, k 3 off dp needle.

BACK::

With size 4 needles, cast on 92 (100, 108) sts. Work in k 2, p 2 ribbing to 3½″, inc 8 sts evenly across last rib row—100 (108, 116) sts. Change to size 6 needles and cable patt.

Rows 1, 5, and 7 right side: P 5 (6, 7), k 6 (cable panel), * p 8 (9, 10), k 6 (cable panel), rep from * to last 5 (6, 7) sts, p 5 (6, 7).

Rows 2, 4, 6, and 8: K 5 (6, 7), p 6, * k 8 (9, 10), p 6, rep from * to last 5 (6, 7) sts, k 5 (6, 7).

Row 3: P 5 (6, 7), C 6, * p 8 (9, 10), C 6, rep from * to last 5 (6, 7). sts, p 5 (6, 7). Rep these 8 rows for patt. Work to 17″ from beg or desired length to underarm, end ready for a right side row.

Shape Armholes: Keeping to patt bind off 6 sts at beg of next 2 rows—88 (96, 104) sts.

Row 3 (dec row): K 2, sl 1, k 1, psso, keeping to patt work to last 4 sts, k 2 tog, k 2.
Rows 4 and 6: P 3, keeping to patt work to last 3 sts, p 3.
Row 5: K 3, keeping to patt work to last 3 sts, k 3.
Rep Rows 3 through 6 for four (six, eight) times more, then rep Row 3 every 6th row three (two, one) times—72 (78, 84) sts. Beg with a p row, work 5 rows even.

Shape Shoulders: Keeping to patt bind off 6 (7, 8) sts at beg of next 2 (4, 6) rows, then bind off 7 (8, 0) sts at beg of next 4 (2, 0) rows. Sl rem 32 (34, 36) sts to a holder for back neck.

FRONT :

Work same as back until there are 10 rows less than back to beg of shoulders—74 (80, 86) sts.

Shape Neck: Keeping to patt work 26 (28, 30) sts, sl center 22 (24, 26) sts to a holder for front neck edge, join a 2nd ball of yarn, work 26 (28, 30) sts. Working both sides at once, dec 1 st at each neck edge every row three times, every other row two times. *At same time* work last armhole dec as on back—20 (22, 24) sts left each side of work. Work until armholes measure same length as back to shoulders. Shape shoulders same as for back.

SLEEVES :

With size 4 needles, cast on 44 (48, 52) sts. Work in k 2, p 2 ribbing to 3½″, inc 12 (11, 10) sts evenly across last rib row—56 (59, 62) sts. Change to size 6 needles and cable patt.
Rows 1, 5, and 7 (right side): P 4, k 6 (cable panel), * p 8 (9, 10), k 6 (cable panel), rep from * to last 4 sts, p 4.
Rows 2, 4, 6, and 8: K 4, p 6, * k 8 (9, 10), p 6, rep from * to last 4 sts, k 4.
Row 3: P 4, C 6, *p 8 (9, 10), C 6, rep from * to last 4 sts, p 4. Rep these 8 rows for patt. Work to 1½″ above rib band. Inc 1 st each end of next row, then every 1 ½ ″ six times more, working

new sts into reverse st st (p side is right side of work)—70 (73, 76) sts. Work even to 17″ from beg, or desired length to underarm. End ready for a right side row.

Shape Cap: Keeping to patt bind off 6 sts at beg of next 2 rows. Rows 3 and 4: Rep Rows 3 and 4 of back armhole shaping—56 (59, 62) sts. Continue to rep Rows 3 and 4 seventeen (eighteen, nineteen) times more. Work 5 rows even. Mark beg and end of next row for start of saddle. Work even until side edges of saddle measure same as shaped shoulder edge. Sl these sts to a holder.

Finishing: Sew side edges of sleeve saddles to front shoulders. Sew or weave sleeves to front armholes. Sew left sleeve saddle to back shoulder. Sew or weave left sleeve to back armhole.

Neckband: From right side, beg at back neck edge with size 4 needles, k 32 (34, 36) sts from back holder, dec 4 sts evenly across to become 28 (30, 32) sts; k 22 (23, 24) sts from left sleeve holder, dec 3 (4, 5) sts evenly across to become 19 sts; pick up 13 sts along left neck edge; k 22 (24, 26) sts from front holder, dec 2 sts evenly across to become 20 (22, 24) sts; pick up 13 sts along right neck edge; k 22 (23, 24) sts from right sleeve holder, dec 3 (4, 5) sts evenly across to become 19 sts—112 (116, 120) sts. Work in k 2, p 2 ribbing to 2½″. Bind off in ribbing. Sew right sleeve saddle to back shoulder. Sew or weave right sleeve to back armhole. Sew side and sleeve seams. Sew neckband tog. Fold neckband in half to inside and sew down. Block.

Blue and Silver Blouse with Silver Disco Bag

Sizes:

Directions are for bust sizes 30″ to 32″. Changes for sizes 34″ to 36″ and 38″ are in parentheses.

Measurements:

Finished width around underarm 33″ (35½″, 38″).

Materials:

Fingering-weight Lurex, 20-gr. balls.

Blouse:
Light Blue (MC)	6 (7, 8)
Silver (CC)	4 (5, 6)

Bag: 1 (CC)

Size D aluminum crochet hook.
½″ Plastic ring.

Needles:

Sizes 3 and 4, or sizes to obtain gauge.

Gauge:

In st st 6 sts = 1″, 8 rows = 1″.
In knit-in patt 7 sts = 1″, 8 rows = 1″.

Note: When changing colors pick up color to be used under color previously used, twisting yarn to prevent holes. Carry color not in use on wrong side of work, being careful to maintain gauge.

BACK:

With size 3 needles and MC, cast on 103 (111, 119) sts.

Row 1 (wrong side): P 1, * k 1, p 1, rep from * to end.

Row 2: K 1, * p 1, k 1, rep from * to end. Rep these 2 rows for rib patt. Work to 3″, inc 1 st at center of last rib row—104 (112, 120) sts. Change to size 4 needles. Join CC. Beg patt following chart. Work to top of chart, then rep these 16 rows for patt throughout. Work to 16″ from beg or desired length to underarm. End ready for a wrong side row.

Shape Armholes: Keeping to patt with MC, cast on 6 sts at end of next 2 rows—116 (124, 132) sts.

Row 3: With MC [p 1, k 1] three times, p 1, keeping to patt work to last 7 sts, with MC p 1, [k 1, p 1] three times.

Row 4: With MC [k 1, p 1], three times, sl 1, k 1, psso, keeping to patt work to last 8 sts, with MC k 2 tog, [p 1, k 1] three times. Rep Rows 3 and 4 fourteen (sixteen, eighteen) times more—86 (90, 94) sts. Rep Row 4 every 4th row nine times—68 (72, 76) sts. Work 3 rows even, ending ready for a right side row. Bind off all sts.

FRONT:

With size 3 needles and MC, cast on 115 (123, 131) sts. Work in rib patt same as back to 3″, inc 1 st at center of last rib row. 116 (124, 132) sts. Change to size 4 needles.

Row 1: With MC [k 1, p 1] three times, beg with Row 1, work in patt following chart over next 104 (112, 120) sts, with MC [p 1, k 1] three times. Working 6 sts at each edge in ribbing with MC, work in patt following chart over rem sts. Work even until front measures same as back to 1 row less than beg of armhole decs. End ready for a wrong side row. Rep Rows 3 and 4 of back armhole shaping fifteen (seventeen, nineteen) times, then rep Row 4 every 4th row three times—80 (84, 88) sts. Work 2 rows, ending ready for a wrong side row.

Shape Neck: Keeping to patt work 30 (31, 32) sts, sl on a holder for right side, bind off center 20 (22, 24) sts, work 30 (31, 32) sts. Continue to dec 1 st at armhole edge as established every 4th row 6 times more, and at *same time* dec 1 st at neck edge every row four times, every other row 5 times—15 (16, 17) sts. Work until armhole measures same as back to shoulders. Bind off all sts. Sl right front sts to a size 4 needle. Work same as left front reversing shaping.

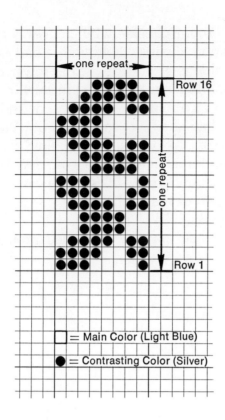

Finishing: Sew left shoulder seam.

Neckband: From right side with size 3 needles and MC, beg at right back neck edge, pick up 111 (115, 119) sts around entire neck edge. Work in k 1, p 1 ribbing for 2″, ending ready for a right side row. Bind off loosely in knit. Sew right shoulder seam. Fold neckband in half to front and sew down. Sew side seams to beg of armholes. Sew back armhole band to inside of front band. Block.

DISCO BAG:

With size 4 needles and CC, cast on 43 sts.
Row 1 (right side): Purl.
Row 2: K 1, * with yarn in front of work (called wyif) sl next st, k 1, rep from * to end.
Row 3: Purl.
Row 4: K 2, wyif sl next st, * k 1, wyif sl next st, rep from * end k 2. Rep these 4 rows for patt. Work to 8½″.

Flap: Keeping to patt, dec 1 st each end of next row, then every other row until 5 sts are left. Bind off.

Finishing: From right side with crochet hook size D, work one row sc around all sides. Fold bag in half to beg of flap, being sure right side is at outside. Beg at lower corner of side edge with D hook sc sides of beg tog to start of flap. *Do not* fasten off; make a ch about 20″ long. Sl st in 2nd ch from hook and each ch to bag of side edge. Fasten off. Work other side edge and tie to correspond. Block bag. Fold flap to front. Using 2 strands of CC crochet around plastic ring. Weave center of ring tog. Sew to front of flap. If desired sew on a snap to inside flap. Sew other part of snap to front.

Note: Disco bag may be worn tied around neck or around waist.

Blue Aran Isle Poncho

Size:

One size fits all (approx 60″ × 46″).

Materials:

55 percent acrylic/45 percent medium-weight bulky wool, 1 ⁷⁄₁₀ oz.-balls, 30 Medium Blue.

Size J aluminum crochet hook.

Needles:

Size 10½ or size to obtain gauge; 1 cable or double-point (dp).

Gauge:

In st st 4 sts = 1″, 5 rows = 1″.
In Aran patts 4 sts = 1″, 5 rows = 1″.

Abbreviations:

6 St Right Cable (called 6 RC): Sl next 3 sts to a dp needle, hold in back of work, k 3, k 3 off dp needle.
6 St Left Cable (called 6 LC): Sl next 3 sts to a dp needle, hold in front of work, k 3, k 3 off dp needle.
2 Twist (called 2 T): Sl next st to a dp needle, hold in front of work, k 1, k 1 off dp needle.
4 St Right Cable (called 4 RC): Sl next 2 sts to a dp needle, hold in back of work, k 2, k 2 off dp needle.
4 St Left Cable (called 4 LC): Sl next 2 sts to a dp needle, hold in front of work, k 2, k 2 off dp needle.

PATT 1:

Garter st worked over given number of sts:
Row 1: K.
Row 2: K. Rep these 2 rows for Patt 1.

PATT 2:

Left Cable worked over 8 sts:
Rows 1 and 5 (right side): P 1, k 6, p 1.

Rows 2, 4, and 6: K 1, p 6, k 1.
Row 3: P 1, 6 LC, p 1. Rep these 6 rows for Patt 2.

PATT 3:

Seed st triangle worked over 11 sts:
Row 1 (right side): K 11.
Row 2: P 5, k 1, p 5.
Row 3: K 4, p 1, k 1, p 1, k 4.
Row 4: P 3, k 1, p 3, k 1, p 3.
Row 5: K 2, p 1, k 5, p 1, k 2.
Row 6: P 1, k 1, p 7, k 1, p 1. Rep these 6 rows for Patt 3.

PATT 4:

Twist st and Hourglass Cable worked over 16 sts.
Row 1 (right side): P 1, 2 T, p 1, k 2, 4 RC, k 2, p 1, 2 T, p 1.
Row 2 and all even rows through 8: On wrong side, k the knit sts
    and p the purl sts.
Row 3: P 1, 2 T, p 1, 4 RC, 4 LC, p 1, 2 T, p 1.
Row 5: P 1, 2 T, p 1, k 8, p 1, 2 T, p 1.
Row 7: P 1, 2 T, p 1, 4 LC, 4 RC, p 1, 2 T, p 1. Rep these 8 rows
    for Patt 4.

PATT 5:

(Seed st diamond worked over 15 sts).
Row 1 (right side): K 7, p 1, k 7.
Row 2: P 6, k 1, p 1, k 1, p 6.
Row 3: K 5, p 1, [k 1, p 1] twice, k 5.
Row 4: P 4, k 1, [p 1, k 1] three times, p 4.
Row 5: K 3, p 1, [k 1, p 1] four times, k 3.
Row 6: P 2, k 1, [p 1, k 1] five times, p 2.
Row 7: Rep Row 5.
Row 8: Rep Row 4.
Row 9: Rep Row 3.
Row 10: Rep Row 2.
Row 11: Rep Row 1.
Row 12: P 15. Rep these 12 rows for Patt 5.

PATT 6:

Right Cable worked over 8 sts:
Rows 1 and 5 (right side): P 1, k 6, p 1.
Rows 2, 4, and 6: K 1, p 6, k 1.
Row 3: P 1, 6 RC, p 1. Rep these 6 rows for Patt 6.

Note: Poncho is worked in two pieces. Each piece begs at lower back and ends at lower front. When completed, pieces are joined at center back and front.

LEFT BACK:

With size 10½ needles, cast on 78 sts. K 8 rows, inc 12 sts evenly across last row—90 sts. Beg Aran patts.

Row 1 (right side): Mark beg of this row for center edge of poncho. Work Row 1 of Patt 2 over 8 sts, Row 1 of Patt 3 over 11 sts, Row 1 of Patt 4 over 16 sts, Row 1 of Patt 5 over 15 sts, Row 1 of Patt 4 over 16 sts, Row 1 of Patt 3 over 11 sts, Row 1 of Patt 2 over 8 sts, Row 1 of Patt 1 over 5 sts.

Row 2: Work Row 2 of Patt 1 over 5 sts, Row 2 of Patt 2 over 8 sts, Row 2 of Patt 3 over 11 sts, Row 2 of Patt 4 over 16 sts, Row 2 of Patt 5 over 15 sts, Row 2 of Patt 4 over 16 sts, Row 2 of Patt 3 over 11 sts, Row 2 of Patt 2 over 8 sts. Keeping to patts as established, work until 13th Row 6 of Patt 5 is completed, ending at center edge.

Shape Neck and Left Front: Bind off 18 sts for back neck edge, and keeping to patt, complete row-72 sts. Work even until 33rd Row 5 of Patt 3 is completed. Keeping to patts work 1 row, ending cast on 18 sts.

Next Row: P 1, k 6, p 1 (These 8 sts were worked in Patt 2 on back. From this point on work these 8 sts in Patt 6, forming first cable twist on same row as cable twist of Patt 2), work Row 1 of Patt 3 over next 11 sts, keeping to patts complete row—90 sts. Work even until 25th Row 12 of Patt 5 is completed. K 1 row, dec 12 sts evenly across. K 7 rows more. Bind off.

RIGHT BACK:

Work same as left back to first patt row.

Row 1 (right side): Work Row 1 of Patt 1 over 5 sts, Row 1 of Patt 6 over 8 sts, Row 1 of Patt 3 over 11 sts, Row 1 of Patt 4 over 16 sts, Row 1 of Patt 5 over 15 sts, Row 1 of Patt 4 over 16 sts, Row 1 of Patt 3 over 11 sts, Row 1 of Patt 6 over 8 sts. Keeping to patts as established, work as left side piece, reversing all shaping until 33rd Row 5 of Patt 3 is completed. At beg of next row cast on 18 sts, and keeping to patts, work to end.

Next Row: Keeping to patts, work to last 19 sts, work Row 1 of Patt 3 over 11 sts, p 1, k 6, p 1 (These 8 sts will now be worked in Patt 2). Complete as left side piece.

Finishing: Weave pieces tog at center front and back.

RIGHT SHAWL COLLAR :

From right side with size 10½ needles, beg lower right front corner of neck. Pick up 41 sts evenly along right front neck edge to back, pick up 18 sts along back neck edge to center seam—59 sts.

Row 1 (wrong side): P 1, * k 1, p 1, rep from * to end.

Row 2: K 1, * p 1, k 1, rep from * to end. Rep these 2 rows for rib patt. Work 2 rows more. Inc 1 st at end of next row, then every 6th row until front side edge measures same as front neck edge, working new sts into rib pat. Bind off in ribbing.

LEFT SHAWL COLLAR :

Beg at back center seam work same as right shawl collar, reversing shaping. Sew lower front edge of right collar to front neck edge; sew lower front edge of left collar to front neck edge inside right collar. Sew collar tog at center back.

BELT :

With crochet hook size J make a ch about 78″ long or desired length. Sl st in 2nd ch from hook and each ch to end. Fasten off.

TASSELS :

Make 2. Cut 10 strands of yarn about 12″ long. Fold strands in half. Wind a separate strand of yarn around tassel about ½″ below loop end. Knot tightly. Sew loop ends of tassels to ends of belt. Trim ends of tassels. Wet block. Do not steam-iron.

Note: Poncho can be worn two ways, loose or sides of front wrapped to center back and belted.

Off-White Shetland Lace Blouson

Sizes:

Directions are for bust size 30″. Changes for sizes 32″, 34″, and 36″ are in parentheses.

Measurements:

Finished width around underarm 34″ (36″, 39″).

Materials:

100 percent Wool, light-weight Shetland-type yarn, 1 ⅝-oz. balls, 6 (7, 8) Off-White.

Size D aluminum crochet hook.

½″ Elastic ribbon.

Needles:

Size 4, or size to obtain gauge.

Gauge:

In st st 6 sts = 1″.
In Lace Patt 17 sts = 3″, 8 rows = 1″.

BACK:

With size 4 needles, cast on 97 (103, 111) sts. Casing: Beg with a p row, work in st st for 13 rows. Beg Lace Patt.

Row 1 (right side): K 6 (6, 7), p 1, * k 5, p 1, rep from *, end k 6 (6, 7).

Row 2: P 6 (6, 7), k 1, * p 5, k 1, rep from *, end p 6 (6, 7).

Row 3: K 1 (1, 2), * yo, sl 1, k 1, psso, p 1, k 2 tog, yo, k 1, rep from * end k 0 (0, 1).

Rows 4, 6, and 8: P 3 (3, 4), k 1, * p 5, k 1, rep from * end p 3 (3, 4).

Rows 5 and 7: K 3 (3, 4), p 1, * k 5, p 1, rep from * end k 3 (3, 4).

Row 9: K 1 (1, 2), k 2 tog, yo, k 1, yo, sl 1, k 1, psso, * p 1, k 2 tog, yo, k 1, yo, sl 1, k 1, psso, rep from *, end k 1 (1, 2).

Rows 10 and 12: Rep Row 2.

Row 11: Rep Row 1. Rep these 12 rows for patt. Work to about 14½" from beg ending with Row 2 or 8 of patt.

Shape Armholes: Keeping to patt bind off 6 (6, 7) sts at beg of next 2 rows. Dec 1 st each end every other row six times—73 (79, 85) sts. Work even in patt until armholes measure 7" (7½"–8"). End ready for a right side row.

Shape Shoulders: Keeping to patt bind off 5 (6, 7) sts beg of next 4 rows, then bind off 7 sts beg of next 2 rows. Bind off rem 39 (41, 43) sts for back neck edge.

FRONT :

Work same as back to beg of armhole shaping.

Shape Armhole and Front Opening: Keeping to patt bind off 6 (6, 7) sts, work until there are 43 (46, 49) sts on right-hand needle. Sl rem sts to a holder to be worked later. Keeping 1 st at front edge in garter st (k every row), work in patt dec 1 st at armhole edge every other row six times—37 (40, 43) sts. Work even until armhole measures 2" (2½", 2¾"), ending at front edge.

Shape Neck: Keeping to patt work 8 (9, 10) sts, sl to a holder for neckband, complete row. Dec 1 st at neck edge every row seven times, every other row five times—17 (19, 21) sts. Work even until armhole measures same as back to shoulder, ending at armhole edge.

Shape Shoulder: Keeping to patt bind off 5 (6, 7) sts every other row two times, then bind off rem 7 sts. Sl sts from holder to a needle. Inc 1 st in first st, keeping to patt complete row. Work to correspond to other side reversing shaping.

SLEEVES:

With size 4 needles cast on 45 (49, 53) sts. Work casing same as on lower back, inc—40 (42, 40) sts evenly across last casing row—85 (91, 93) sts. Beg with Row 1 of back, work in Lace Patt. Work 6 rows. Dec 1 st each end of next row then every 6th row five times more, every 12th row three (three, two) times—67 (73, 77) sts. Work even to about 19" from beg or 2" more than desired length, ending with Row 2 or 8 of patt.

Shape Cap: Keeping to patt bind off 6 (6, 7) sts at beg of next 2 rows. Dec 1 st each end every row four times, every other row thirteen (fourteen, fifteen) times. Bind off 2 sts at beg of next 4 rows. Bind off rem sts.

Finishing: Sew shoulder side and sleeve seams. Sew in sleeves.

NECKBAND:

From right side sl 8 (9, 10) right front sts from holder to a needle. With same needle pick up 35 sts along right neck edge, pick up 39 (41, 43) sts along back neck edge, pick up 35 sts along left neck edge, k 8 (9, 10) sts from left front holder—125 (129, 133) sts. Beg with a p row. Work in st st for 11 rows. Bind off. From right side beg at top left corner of neckband, with D crochet hook work 1 row sc down left front opening and up right front opening to top of neckband. Fasten off. Fold neckband in half to wrong side. Sew down leaving an opening at each front edge. Along lower edge of body and sleeves fold casings in half to wrong side. Sew down leaving an opening for elastic. Cut elastic ribbon to desired hip and wrist sizes. Weave through casings. Sew end of elastic tog. Sew up opening.

Neck Tie: With D crochet hook make a ch about 50″ long. Sl st in 2nd ch from hook and each ch to end. Fasten off. Beg and ending at front edge weave tie through neckband. Block.

Monna Weinman

Monna Weinman, born in Austria and trained in knitting in the best European tradition, is truly one of the great knitters working today. Before coming to this country to settle permanently, Monna designed and manufactured hand-knitted and hand-crocheted garments for London's foremost department stores—Fortnum & Mason, Marshall & Snellgrove, and Harrods. She also designed for top European fashion publications including Vogue and Harper's Bazaar.

Two weeks after arriving in the United States, Monna began working as a designer for Coats & Clark, which she continued to do for almost a decade. Turning to free-lance work, she designed for the Vogue Knitting Book (until its demise) and for most of the major fashion and crafts magazines. She continues to work for a large number of yarn companies and her designs are seen regularly in Ladies' Home Journal Needle & Craft, Woman's Day, Family Circle, and other top magazines.

"My most enjoyable memories in all the years that I've been knitting have to do with the time when I employed and taught blind people how to knit. That was many years ago in London, during the Second World War. They were wonderful people and wonderful knitters. And they loved their work. The things we made we sold to the best stores in London. And, strangely enough, because of their handicap the sweaters my knitters made were the best sweaters in London. In those days everything was rationed and you weren't allowed to use too much yarn or too many buttons. But my knitters were allowed to use all the yarn they wanted and as many buttons as they wanted. So you could tell our sweaters from everyone else's: Ours were the ones with lots of buttons. Times were hard then for everybody, but we still had lots of fun together.

"There's something I recommend for knitters today that's almost as scarce today as buttons were during those days in London: plastic knitting needles. Old bone or ivory needles are almost easier to come by. I always knit with plastic needles, never with the steel kind. Plastic needles give a little in your hands and that's better for your fingers than steel needles, which are too firm for me. But it seems as if only steel ones are made now. If you know of anyone who has some plastic needles they don't want, let me know."

Monna Weinman

Man's Vest

Sizes:

Directions are for size 38. Changes for sizes 40 and 42 are in parentheses.

Measurements:

Finished 40" (42", 44").

Materials:

Sport-weight yarn, 2-oz. skeins, 5 (6, 7).
6 Buttons.

Needles:

1 pair each of sizes 5 and 7.

Pattern Stitch:

Multiple of 6 + 2.
Row 1: Knit.
Row 2: K 2, * p 4, k 2. Rep from * across.
Rows 3 and 4: Rep Rows 1 and 2.
Row 5: Knit.
Row 6: P 3, * k 2, p 4. Rep from * to last 3 sts, k 3.
Rows 7 and 8: Rep Rows 5 and 6.

BACK:

With size 5 needles, cast on 97 (103, 109) sts. Work in ribbing of k 1, p 1 for 2", inc 1 st at end of last row. Change to size 7 needles and work in patt on 98 (104, 110) sts until piece measures 15½" (16", 16½").

Armholes: Bind off 7 sts at the beg of next 2 rows. Bind off 3 sts at the beg of following 2 rows. Dec 1 st both ends every other row two (two, three) times. Work on rem 74 (80, 84) sts until armholes measure 9½" (10", 10").

Shoulders: Bind off 7 (8, 9) sts at the beg of next 6 rows. Bind off rem 32 (32, 30) sts.

RIGHT FRONT:

With size 5 needles, cast on 57 (57, 63) sts. Work in ribbing for 2″. Change to size 7 needles and work as follows:

Row 1: K 1, (p 1, k 1) three times, k across.

Row 2: K 2, * p 4, k 2 rep from * to last 7 sts, p 1, (k 1, p 1) three times. Work in patt, keeping the 7 sts for front border in ribbing until piece measures 15½″ (16″, 16½″), ending with wrong side facing.

Armhole and Neck Shaping: Bind off 7 sts at the beg of next row. Work to end.

Next row: Rib 7, k 2 tog through back of sts, neckshaping. Work in patt to end of row.

Following row: Bind off 3 sts at the beg of row. Work to end. Dec. 1 st at armhole edge every other row two (two, three) times. At the same time dec 1 st at neck edge as before, after the front border, every 4th row twelve (ten, twelve) times more. Then dec 1 st at same edge every other row four (three, three) times. Work on rem 28, (31, 34) sts until armhole measures 9½″ (10″, 10″). End at armhole edge.

Shoulder: Bind off 7 (8, 9) sts every other row three times. Work on rem 7 sts in ribbing until piece reaches to center of back of neck. Bind off.

Position of Buttonholes: With pins mark the position of 6 buttons on right front band, having the first pin mark ½″ from lowered edge and the last pin mark ½″ from neck shaping.

LEFT FRONT:

Work as for right front, reversing patt and shapings and knitting 2 tog through front of sts when dec for neck shaping. Work a buttonhole opposite each pin mark as follows: Work to last 5 sts, k 2 tog, yo, rib 3 sts.

RIGHT POCKET:

With size 7 needles, cast on 28 sts. Work in patt as follows:

Row 1: Knit.

Row 2: P 1, * k 2, p 4. Rep from * three times, k 2, p 1.

Rows 3 and 4: Rep Rows 1 and 2.

Row 5: Knit.

Row 6: * P 4, k 2. Rep from * three times, p 4.

Rows 7 and 8: Rep Rows 5 and 6. Work until piece measures 3½″. End with wrong side facing.

Next row: Bind off 12 sts at the beg of row. Work to end.

Following row: K across to last 2 sts, k 2 tog. Dec 1 st a same edge every row until all sts are worked off. Break off. With right side facing and size 5 needle pick up and knit 33 sts along the shaped part of pocket. Starting with a purl st, work in ribbing for 5 rows. Bind off in ribbing. Work other pocket to correspond, reversing shapings.

Armband: Sew shoulder seams. With right side facing, on size 5 needles pick up and knit 132 (138, 138) sts along armhole edge. Work in ribbing for 5 rows. Bind off in ribbing.

Finishing: Sew side seams. Sew on pockets as illustrated. Sew on buttons.

Blouse with Ruffles

Size:

Directions are given for size 10. Changes for sizes 12 and 14 are in parentheses.

Measurements:

Finished bust 34″ (36″, 38″).

Materials:

3-ply Fingering yarn, 1-oz. skeins, 9 (9, 10).

Size E aluminum crochet hook.

½″ Elastic.

Needles:

Sizes 4 and 6.

Gauge:

6 sts = 1″ on size 6 needles.

Pattern Stitch:

Multiple of 6 +1.
Row 1: * K 1, yo, sl 1, k 1, psso, k 1, k 2 tog, yo. Rep from * to last st, k 1.
Row 2 and all even rows: Purl.
Row 3: * K 2, yo, k 3, yo, k 1. Rep from * to last st, k 1.
Row 5: K 2 tog, * yo, sl 1, k 1, psso, k 1, k 2 tog, yo, sl 1, k 2 tog, psso. Rep from *, end, sl 1, k 1, psso, instead of sl 1, k 2 tog, psso.
Row 7: * K 1, k 2 tog, yo, k 1, yo, sl 1, k 1, psso, rep from * to last st, k 1.
Row 9: Rep Row 3.
Row 11: * K 1, k 2 tog, yo, sl 1, k 2 tog, psso, yo, sl 1, k 1 psso. Rep from * to last st, k 1.
Row 12: Purl.

Note: There are 2 sts more for each patt on Rows 3 and 9.

BACK:

With size 4 needles, cast on 91 (97, 103) sts. Work in st st for 7 rows. Next row, (hemline): K across. Change to size 6 needles and work in patt having on Row 3 and Row 9 121 (129, 137) sts. Work until piece measures from hemline 14″ (14″, 14½″), ending with either Row 5 or 11.

Armholes: Bind off 5 (6, 6) sts at beg of next 2 rows. Bind off 2 (2, 3) sts at the beg of following 2 rows. Dec. 1 st at same edge once. Work on rem 75 (79, 83) sts until armholes measure 5″ (5½″, 6″), end with row 5 or 11.

Neck Shaping: Work across first 29 (30, 31) sts, bind off next 17 (19, 21) sts, work across last 29 (30, 31) sts. Work on last set of sts only, binding off 6 sts at neck edge once. Dec 1 st at neck edge every other row 2 (3, 4) times. Work on rem 21 sts until armhole measures 7″ (7½″, 8″,) ending at armhole edge.

Shoulder: Bind off 7 sts every other row three times. Attach yarn to neck edge of other part and work to correspond with first part.

FRONT:

Work as for back until armholes measure 3″ (3½″, 4″). End with Row 5 or 11.

Neck Shaping and Shoulders: Work as for back.

SLEEVES:

With size 4 needles, cast on 73 (79, 85) sts. Work in st st for 7 rows.
Next row, (hemline): Knit. Change to size 6 needles and work in patt until piece measures from hemline 14″ (14″, 14½″).
End with Row 5 or 11.

Shape Top: Bind off 5 (6, 6) sts at the beg of next 2 rows. Bind off 2 (2, 3) sts, at the beg of following 2 rows. Dec 1 st both ends of every other row five (five, six,) times. Dec 1 st both ends every row until piece measures 3½″, (4″, 4½″). Bind off 2 sts beg. of next 2 rows. Bind off rem sts.

Neckband: Sew right shoulder seam. With size 4 needles and right side of work facing, pick up and k 174 (180, 184) sts. Work in ribbing of k 1, p 1, for 5 rows. Bind off in ribbing.

Ruffle: With size 4 needles, cast on 7 sts.

Row 1: K 4, yo, sl 1, k 1, psso, yo, k 1, (8 sts)

Row 2 and all even rows: Purl to last 2 sts, k 2.

Row 3: K 2, k 2 tog, yo, k 3, yo, k1. (9 sts)

Row 5: K 4, yo, sl 1, k 2 tog, psso, yo, sl 1, k 1, psso. (8 sts).

Row 6: Bind off 1 st, p 4, k 2. (7 sts). Work in patt until piece when gathered reaches around entire neck edge. Bind off. Work same ruffle for each sleeve until piece measures 13½″ (14″, 15″). Bind off.

Finishing: Sew left shoulder seam and ribbing. Sew side seams. Turn under hem and stitch in place. Gather ruffle for neck line and sew in place, leaving ribbing free. Sew short end of ruffle. Turn under hem of sleeves and sew in place. Sew lace to bottom of sleeve, without gathering it. Draw elastic through hem. Sew short ends of elastic together. Sew side seams of sleeves. Sew in sleeves.

Cord: With double strand of yarn make a chain of desired length. Sl st in 2nd ch from hook and each ch across. Draw cord through holes of pattern.

Entrelacs or
Trellis Sweater

Size:

Directions are for size 34″ (knitted measurements 36″), knitted on size 8 double-pointed needles. For size 32″ (knitted measurements 34″), use same instructions using size 7 needles; for size 36″ (knitted measurements 38″), use size 9 needles.

Materials:

100 percent knitting worsted wool, 4-oz. balls.

4 Balls of Main Color (MC).

1 Ball each of Contrasting Colors (CCA) and (CCB).

Needles:

1 pair size 7; 10 double-pointed size 8; circular size 7.

Gauge:

On size 8 needles in st st: 5 sts = 1″.

BACK:

With MC and size 8 needles, cast on 64 sts. Work first row of triangles as follows: * P 2; turn, k these 2 sts; turn, p 3, turn, k 3; turn, p 4; turn, k 4; turn; cont in this way until you have 8 sts on right-hand needle. Leave these sts on dp needle. Without breaking yarn, rep from * seven times more. You have completed the first row of triangles which will be the base on which you will begin the first row of rectangles.

First Row of Rectangles: With CCB, k 2; turn, p 2; turn, inc 1 st in 1st st, sl 1 as if to k, k 1, psso, skpo, turn, p 3; turn, inc 1 st in 1st st, k 1, skpo; turn, p 4; turn. Cont in this way until you have used up all the sts (in MC) of the first base triangle. Break off yarn. Leave the sts in CCB on dp needle. * With CCA pick up and k 8 sts along left edge of first triangle, turn and p these 8 sts; turn, k 7; skpo. The st slipped is the last of the 8 sts picked up and the k st is the first of the following triangle; turn, p 8; turn, k 7; skpo, turn, p 8; turn. Cont in this way until all sts in

198

MC of the next triangle have been used up. Break off CCA. With CCB rep from *. Work in this manner, alternating CCB with CCA three times in all. Work one rectangle with CCA. You have worked off all sts in MC and have 8 sts on each of the 8 needles. With CCB and 9th dp needle, pick up and k 8 sts along left edge of last triangle; turn, p 2 tog; p 6; turn, k 7; turn, p 2 tog; p 5, turn, k 6; turn. Cont in same way until 1 st remains. The first row of multicolored rectangles is completed.

Second Row of Rectangles: With MC, k the last rem sts; turn. Pick up and p 7 sts along straight edge of triangle just completed; turn, * k 8; turn, p 7, p 2 tog using the last st of the 8 sts picked up and the first st on dp needle of next rectangle; turn, k 8, turn, p 7; p 2 tog; turn. Cont in this way until all sts in CCA have been used up. Do not break yarn. Working with MC only, pick up and p 8 sts along side of next rectangle Rep from * seven times.

Third Row of Rectangles: With CCA k 2; turn, p 2, turn, inc 1 st in first st, skpo, turn, p 3; turn, inc 1 st in first st, k 1, skpo; turn, p 4, turn. Cont in this way as for first row of rectangles, but reversing colors, starting with CCA then using CCB and ending with CCA.

Fourth Row of Rectangles: With MC work as for second row of rectangles. The last 4 rows form the color patt. Work until 15 rows of rectangles have been completed. With MC work a row of triangles as follows: There is 1 st on left-hand needle. * pick up and p 7 sts along side of last rectangle, turn, k 8; turn, p 2 tog. p 5; p 2 tog using the last st on needle and the first st of following rectangle, turn, k 7; turn, p 2 tog, p 4, p 2 tog; turn, k 6; turn. Cont in this way until 1 st remains. Rep from * seven times. With right side facing and MC and size 8 needles pick up and k 64 sts along top of back. Inc 1 sc in last st. P 1 row—65 sts.

SHOULDERS:

Bind off 5 sts at beg of next 4 rows. Bind off 4 sts at beg of following 2 rows. Place rem 37 sts on dp needle. With right side facing, MC and size 7 needles, pick up and k 81 sts along bottom of back. Work in ribbing of k 1, p 1 for 21 rows. Bind off loosely in ribbing.

FRONT:

Work as for back until 2 rows in MC and st st have been completed.

Shoulders and Neckshaping: Bind off 5 sts at the beg of next row, k across next 12 sts, turn. Bind off 2 sts at beg of following row, neck edge, p to end.
Next row: Bind off 5 sts beg of row, k to last 2 sts, k 2 tog. P 1 row. Bind off rem 4 sts. Place center 31 sts on dp needle, attach yarn to next st and work other side to correspond.

SLEEVES:

With MC and size 7 needles, cast on 49 sts. Work in ribbing of k 1, p 1, inc 1 st every 6th row twenty-one times. Work on 91 sts until piece measures 19″, or desired length. Bind off loosely in ribbing.

COLLAR:

Sew shoulder seams. With right side of work and MC, k across the 37 sts of neck of back, inc 9 sts evenly across—46 sts. Pick up and k 6 sts along shaped edge of front, k across 31 center sts, inc 7 sts evenly across,—38 sts. Pick up and k 6 sts along other shaped edge of neck. Change to circular needle and work in ribbing for 8½″. Bind off loosely in ribbing.

Finishing: Fasten off all hanging yarns. Sew side seams to within 8″ from shoulders. Sew sleeve seams. Sew in sleeves.

Man's Fair Isle
Sweater

Size:

Directions are for chest sizes 30″ to 32″. Changes for sizes 34″ to 36″, and 38″, and 42″ to 44″ are in parentheses.

Materials:

Bulky-weight yarn, 6 (6, 7, 8) skeins of Mains Color (MC); 1 skein each of Contrasting Colors (CCA) and (CCB); two long stitch holders.

Needles:

Sizes 8 and 10 double-pointed (dp); sizes 8 and 10 circular.

Gauge:

On size 10 needles: 7 sts = 2″; 5 rounds = 1″. Garment is loose fitting.

Note: Wind patt colors into small balls. Change colors on wrong side, lock strands by picking up new color from under dropped color. Carry colors not used loosely across back of work.

BODY:

Front and back are done in one piece. With MC and size 8 circular needle, cast on 108 (112, 122, 132) sts. Keep a marker on needle between last and first st of rnd. Join. Work in ribbing of k 1, p 1 for 2½″.

Next round: K and inc 1 st in every 7th st six (four, fourteen, twelve) times, then every 11th, (6th, 6th 8th) st six (fourteen, four, six) times. There are on needle 120 (130, 140, 150) sts. Change to size 10 circular needle and k 1 rnd. If border patt is desired, follow chart 1, work patt in st st, k each rnd, beg on Rnd 1. Rep patt to end of rnd. Work to top of chart. Cut off colors CCA and CCB. Change to MC. If border patt is not desired, work with MC only. Mark 60th (65th, 70th, 75th) st for right side seam. With MC work in st st inc 1 st at left side seam

202

(end of rnd) and right side seam every 2 " five times. Work in st st on 130 (140, 150, 160) sts until piece measure 15" (15½", 16", 16") to underarm. Mark 60th (65th, 70th, 75th) st for right side seam. With MC work in st st inc 1 st at left side seam (end of rnd) and right side seam every 2" five times. Work in st st on 130 (140, 150, 160) sts until piece measures 15" (15½", 16", 16") to underarm. In both cases work in st st until piece measures 15" (15½", 16", 16") to underarm.

Next round: Bind off 10 sts underarm, k 55 (60, 65, 70) sts, and put on holder for front; bind off next 10 sts underarm, k to end of rnd; put 55 (60, 65, 70) sts on holder for back.

SLEEVES:

With MC and size 8 dp needles, cast on 28 (34, 40, 46) sts. Divide sts on 3 needles. Mark ends of rnds. Join and work in ribbing of k 1, p 1 for 2½".

Next round: K and inc 12 (6, 10, 4) sts evenly spaced on rnd. There are 40 (40, 50, 50) sts on needles. Change to size 10 dp needles and k 1 rnd. If desired work border patt, following chart 1 for 10 rnds. If border patt is not desired, work with MC only. In both cases work in st st inc 1 st at beg and end of next rnd and every 1½" seven times. Work on 54 (54, 64, 64) sts until piece measures 16" (16½", 17", 17½"). Inc in last row.

Next round: K to within 5 sts of end of rnd, bind off 10 sts underarm, put rem 45 (45, 55, 55) sts on a colored strand of yarn. Work other sleeve same way.

YOKE:

From right side put on size 10 circular needle sts of front, one sleeve, back, and other sleeve. There are on needle 200 (210, 240, 250) sts. With MC work in st st for 3 (5, 6, 7) rnds. Mark ends of rnds.

Pattern: Following chart 1, work in patt, beg at Rnd 1 until 10th rnd has been completed.

Next round: With MC only, * k 3, k 2 tog. Rep from * arnd. Work on rem 160 (168, 192, 200) sts for 1 rnd. Following chart 2 work in patt beg with Rnd 1 until top of chart is reached—13th rnd has been completed. With MC work as follows: * K 1, k 2 tog, k 3, k 2 tog. Rep from * arnd. Work 1 rnd on rem 120 (126, 144, 150) sts. Work in patt 3, following chart for 6 rnds.

Next round: With MC only, work as follows: * K 1, k 2 tog. Rep from * arnd. (There remain 80 (84, 96, 100) sts. Work 1 more rnd with MC. With CCA, k 1 rnd. With CCB, k 1 rnd.

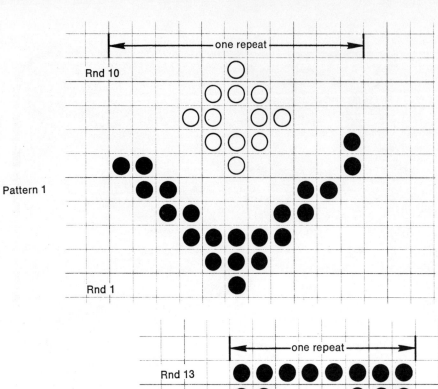

one repeat

Rnd 10

Pattern 1

Rnd 1

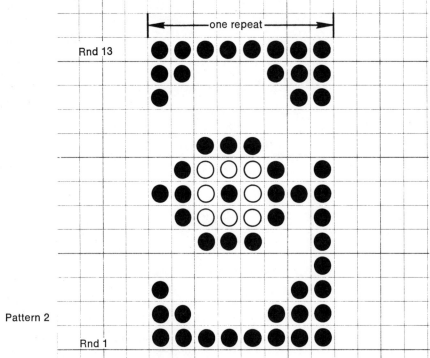

one repeat

Rnd 13

Pattern 2

Rnd 1

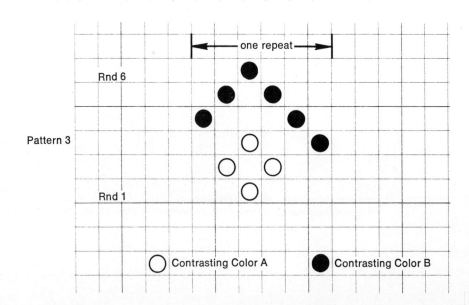

one repeat

Rnd 6

Pattern 3

Rnd 1

○ Contrasting Color A   ● Contrasting Color B

LONG-RIBBED COLLAR OR HOOD:

> For all sizes, with MC and size 8 circular needle, work in ribbing for 12". Bind off loosely in ribbing.

SHORT COLLAR:

> With MC and size 8 circular needle, work as follows: Sizes 30" to 32", * k 2 tog, k 2. Rep from * nineteen times—60 sts. Sizes 34" to 36", k 4, * k 2 tog, k 2. Rep from * nineteen times—64 sts. Sizes 38"to 40", * k 2 tog, k 2. Rep from * thirty-one times—64 sts. Sizes 42" to 44", k 4, * k 2 tog k 2. Rep from * thirty-one times—68 sts. Change to size 8 dp needles and work in ribbing for 3". Bind off loosely in ribbing. Fold ribbing in half and sew in place.

> *Finishing:* Weave bound-off underarm sts. tog. Steam sweater lightly on wrong side.

CAP:

> With MC and size 8 dp needles, cast on 80 sts. Divide sts on 3 needles and mark ends of rnds. Join and work in ribbing of k 1, p 1 for 5½". K for 1 rnd. Work in patt, following chart 1 for 10 rnds. With MC k 1 rnd.

Next round: Slip last st of 3rd needle onto 1st needle, k 3 tog, k 7. Rep from * seven times. With MC work 1 more rnd. Then work 1 rnd in CCA and 1 rnd in CCB. With MC only, k 1 rnd.

Next round: *K 2, k 2 tog. Rep from * arnd. Work 3 rnds on rem 48 sts.

Next round: * K 1, k 2 tog. Rep from * arnd. Work on rem 36 sts for 2 rnds.

Next round: * K 2 tog. Rep from * arnd. Work 1 rnd on 16 sts. Break off, leaving a 10"yarn. Draw yarn through rem sts. Pull tightly and fasten off.

Appendix

The following is a list of projects in which special or unusual yarns were used. Yarns noted are not necessarily the only ones used in the projects mentioned.

Marianne Ake

Rose Chenille Vest (page 4):   6-cut cotton chenille from Coulter Studios.

Blue Linen Lace Pullover (page 7):   Frederick J. Fawcett, size 5/2 slubby linen.

White and Green Blouson with Flowers (page 10):   Candide lightweight wool.

White and Gray Double-Breasted Coat with Shawl Collar (page 15):   Candide heavyweight knitting worsted.

Diamond-Patterned Mohair Pullover in Nine Colors (page 21):   Joseph Galler Majestic Mohair.

Barbara Baker

Man's Alpaca V-Neck Pullover (page 33):   Plymouth Indiecita alpaca, worsted weight.

Woman's Rainbow Popcorn Pullover (page 37):   Manos del Uruguay hand-spun and hand-dyed variegated wool, worsted weight.

Phoebe Fox

Man's Beige-tone Raglan Pullover (page 87):

Tahki Donegal Tweed homespun, bulky weight; Stanley Berroco Dji Dji variegated brushed wool, 77 percent wool–23 percent nylon.

Maria Hart

Klee Sweater (page 107):

Stanley Berroco Dji Dji variegated brushed wool, 77 percent wool–23 percent nylon.

Mohair Dress (page 125):

Stanley Berroco brushed wool, lightweight; Stanley Berroco Mirabella, 87 percent wool–13 percent nylon, lightweight; Stanley Berroco Multiglo, 80 percent wool–20 percent viscose, medium-weight boucle.

Striped Gray Pullover (page 131):

Stanley Berroco Dji Dji variegated brushed wool, 77 percent wool–23 percent nylon, lightweight mohair.

Linda Mendelson

Lacy Armor Vest (page 140):

Tahki heavyweight home-spun sheep's wool.

Bias-knit Geometric Vest (page 143):

Paternayan Pat-Rug, 100 percent wool.

Boat-Neck Sweater (page 146):

Paternayan tapestry yarn, 100 percent wool.

Jacket with Big Sleeves (page 149):

Paternayan Pat-Rug, 100 percent wool.

Rainbow Coat (page 154):

Peternayan Persian yarn, 100 percent wool; Paternayan Pat-Rug, 100 percent wool.

Andrée Rubin

Gold Donegal Tweed Aran Isle Hooded Jacket (page 162):

Tahki Donegal Tweed homespun.

Gray Shetland Cable Sweater with Saddle Shoulders (page 168):

William Unger and Co., Britania.

Blue and Silver Blouse with Silver Disco Bag (page 172):

William Unger and Co., Ariane.

Blue Aran Isle Poncho
(page 177):

William Unger and Co., Fisherknit.

Off-White Shetland Lace
Blouson (page 182):

Spinnerin, Pippin.

Monna Weinman

Man's Fair Isle Sweater
(page 202):

Reynolds Lopi 100 percent wool, worsted
weight.

Sources

Stanley Berroco, Inc.
140 Mendon Street
Uxbridge, MA 10569

Candide Yarns
Main Street
Woodbury, CT 06798

Coulter Studios
118 East 59th Street
New York, NY 10022

Frederick J. Fawcett, Inc.
129 South Street
Boston, MA 02111

Joseph Galler, Inc.
149 Fifth Avenue
New York, NY 10010

Manos del Uruguay
366 Fifth Avenue
New York, NY 10001

Paternayan Brothers, Inc.
312 East 95th Street
New York, NY 10028

Plymouth Yarn Co.
Box 28
Bristol, PA 19007

Reynold Yarns, Inc.
15 Ozer Avenue
Hauppauge, NY 11787

Tahki Imports
62 Madison Street
Hackensack, NJ 07601

William Unger & Co., Inc.
230 Fifth Avenue
New York, NY 10001